Happy Christmas
To the Reynolds family from
A memento of your [...]
from Harold and Pattie Ann
Dec 1999

LIONSGATE

LILIA D'ACRES
DONALD LUXTON

# LIONS GATE

TALONBOOKS

Copyright © 1999  Lilia D'Acres and Donald Luxton

Talonbooks
#104—3100 Production Way
Burnaby, British Columbia, Canada V5A 4R4

Typeset in Garamond and printed and bound in Hong Kong by Kings Time Industries Ltd.

First Printing: August 1999

Talonbooks are distributed in Canada by General Distribution Services,
325 Humber College Blvd., Toronto, Ontario, Canada M9W 7C3; Tel.:(416) 213-1919; Fax:(416) 213-1917.

Talonbooks are distributed in the U.S.A. by General Distribution Services Inc., 4500 Witmer Industrial Estates, Niagara Falls, NY,
U.S.A. 14305-1386. Tel.:1-800-805-1083; Fax:1-800-481-6207.

The publisher gratefully acknowledges the financial support of the Canada Council for the Arts; the Government of Canada through
the Book Publishing Industry Development Program; and the Province of British Columbia through the British Columbia Arts
Council for our publishing activities.

Canadian Cataloguing in Publication Data

D'Acres, Lilia, 1941-
        Lions Gate

        Includes bibliographic references.
        ISBN 0-88922-416-1

        1. Lions Gate Bridge (Vancouver, B.C.)--History.  2. Vancouver
(B.C.)--History.  3. Vancouver (B.C.)--Buildings, structures, etc.  I.
Luxton, Donald, 1954-  II. Title.
FC3847.67.D32 1999          388.1'32'0971133  C99-910802-6
F1089.5.V22D32 1999

Book Design by Leon Phillips.

To Bryn
Who *'plant(s) love among 's'*—*Coriolanus*
Thanks with love L D'A

To DBG from DBL
Couldn't have done it without you

## PHOTOGRAPHERS

**Leonard Frank**: 10, 19 (top), 21, 35, 43, 47, 51 (centre), 58-59, 60-61, 73, 77 (top and bottom), 78 (top), 83, 86 (top), 87 (top), 92, 97, 108 (top, centre and bottom), 116 (bottom), 117, 121 (bottom), 134 (top), 176. **David Loughnan:** 12-13, 67 (top and bottom), 69 (top), 70 (centre left, centre right and bottom), 72 (top and bottom), 74 (bottom), 76 (top and bottom), 79, 80 (centre), 82 (top), 84, 86 (bottom), 88, 90 (top and bottom), 91, 94, 95 (bottom), 96 (top), 103, 106 (top), 118. **Ken Pattison, Photocraft**: 55, 134 (bottom), 135. **James Crookall**: 4-5, 68 (top), 69 (bottom), 70, 74 (centre right), 85 (top and bottom), 87 (bottom), 95, 96 (bottom), 107, 122-123, 125, 129, 166-167 (background). **George Smith**: 89, 98 (top), 102, 111, 115. **J. Sibbald Dow**: 32, 68 (bottom). **W.J. Moore**: 57. **Stuart Thomson**: 120 (top). **Kathleen Taylor**: 23. **Eliza Massey Photography**: 161 (bottom right), 162.

## QUOTES

Douglas Coupland, *This Bridge is Ours:* 9, 163. E. Pauline Johnson-Tekahionwake, *Legends of Vancouver:* 10. Jack Scott, *Suburb in the Sky:* 49. Dennis Fitzgerald, *The Properties:* 51. Roger Smithells, *A Home in the Sky:* 59. Charles Lugrin Shaw, *Spider Web in Steel:* 62, 102, 103. Frank De West, *Vancouver's Lions' Gate Bridge:* 65 (centre), 72, 127 (top). Frederic Mullally, *The Silver Salver:* 127 (centre). *Vancouver Province,* February 28, 1975: 130 (left).

## A NOTE ON SPELLING

The name Lions Gate Bridge rather than the more familiar Lions' Gate Bridge has been consistently used in this text. Newspaper accounts and public documents were inconsistent but generally used the possessive case, and there is no definitive source for the spelling. Although the First Narrows was most commonly known as Lions' Gate, to symbolize the relationship with the North Shore Mountains, the name was never officially adopted. When it was time to finally choose a name for the bridge, the First Narrows Bridge Company dropped the apostrophe, possibly to signify the importance of their own Lions. Recently the Province of British Columbia officially adopted the name Lions Gate Bridge. The final word belongs to Vancouver's always opinionated first archivist, Major Matthews: 'Lions Gate? Good for tourists: no good for practical men. Silly name suitable for romancers.'

# CONTENTS

*Perhaps in your city there is a structure so potent and glorious that its existence in your mind becomes the actual architecture of your mind—a structure through which all of your dreams and ideas and hopes are funneled. In my city, Vancouver, there is one such structure, a fairy-tale bridge called Lions Gate Bridge.*

*We tolerate goodness knows how much from the people and things we love. I figure I have driven across the bridge maybe five or six thousand times in my life—that's all the way from Vancouver to Halifax and back—and never in all of those miles have I once tired of the view, endlessly renewing, endlessly glorious... the bridge's very existence is a metaphor for journey.*

*Here is where civilization ends. Here is where time ends and where eternity begins. Here is Lions Gate Bridge, one last grand gesture of beauty, of charm and of grace before we enter the hinterlands—before the air becomes too brittle and too cold to breathe, before we enter that place where life becomes harsh, and where we must become animals in order to survive.*

*This is what I figure: if there is a heaven, and if heaven has a bridge to take us there, then surely that bridge is Lions Gate Bridge. And this bridge is ours.*

Douglas Coupland

"The Lions"                                                    Copyright Canada 1919

*You can see them as you look towards the north and the west, where the dream-hills swim into the sky amid their ever-drifting clouds of pearl and grey. They catch the earliest hint of sunrise, they hold the last colour of sunset. Twin mountains they are, lifting their twin peaks above the fairest city in all Canada, and known throughout the British Empire as "The Lions of Vancouver."*

E. Pauline Johnson-Tekahionwake

# PREFACE

PARIS HAS THE EIFFEL TOWER. London has Big Ben, San Francisco the Golden Gate Bridge, and New York the Statue of Liberty. Vancouver's icon is the Lions Gate Bridge.

Conceived as a link between the growing City of Vancouver, established on the south side of Burrard Inlet, and large tracts of undeveloped land on the North Shore of this natural harbour, its original function was quite prosaic: to carry traffic across the entrance to this harbour, traditionally known as First Narrows. But the bridge's superbly articulated design provides much more than just a successful resolution of the daunting engineering requirements posed by its construction: it is a consummate union of site and artifact, structure and function, purpose and design, in which utility and beauty are combined in unsurpassed purity of form. It profoundly reconciles nature with human enterprise. This marvel of engineering is also a sublimely beautiful structure.

The Lions Gate Bridge is even more remarkable for having been financed entirely by private capital during the Great Depression. The combined investment of three Guinness brothers bought over 4,000 acres of land in West Vancouver, and financed the bridge that opened this land to development. Even today, just over a third of these lands have been sold, and the remainder is still owned by the successors to the original company.

The impact of these developments on the city and its inhabitants was phenomenal, and the bridge's success soon led to talk of its obsolescence. Just seventeen years after completion, it was bought by the Province of British Columbia, and discussions began on whether or not to alter, revamp or replace this landmark structure. For decades the bridge deteriorated visibly as its maintenance was neglected. Thirty-eight years passed, by which time replacement was considered essential, and the province set out to determine its most suitable form. Public opinion was split along clearly defined lines of self-interest, and the debate raged on for another five years. This issue polarized visions for the City's future: one which saw further opportunities for the growth of traffic; and another which proposed limits to the expansion of the role of the automobile in the city.

In 1998, after forty-three years of debate, the Province of British Columbia finally decided to abandon plans to demolish or significantly alter the Lions Gate Bridge. Its three lane configuration would be retained and widened. The bridge would be rescued and renewed, and would continue to grace the entrance to Vancouver's harbour into the new century.

What has often been forgotten or misunderstood during these decades of debate was how and why the bridge was built. It is a story of hubris and ego, shameless greed, relentless promotion, backroom deals, political influence and interference, the final throes of the British Empire, the destruction of national economies through the birth of a new, multinational ruling class, and of profound personal triumph and tragedy. To build such a structure, in a frontier city during the deepest depression of the twentieth century, was an uncompromising act of iron wills—a clash of titans. This story deserves to be told.

# PART ONE

*Some day, mark my words, there'll be a bridge across this point.*
George Grant Mackay, 1890

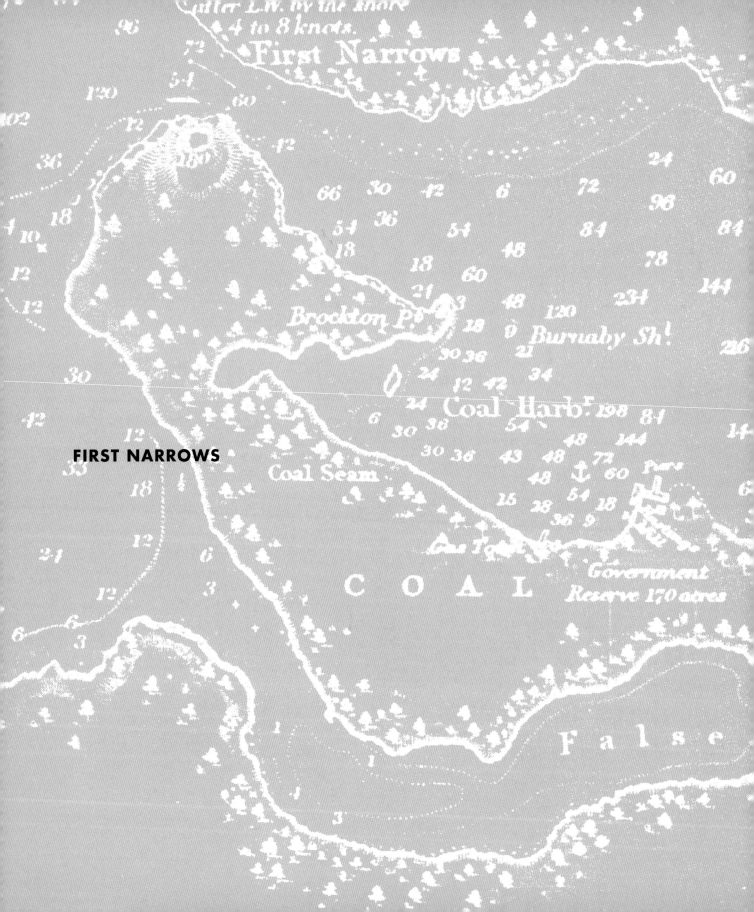

FIRST NARROWS

VANCOUVER AND ITS HARBOUR are one. The city was built to provide a terminus for a new transcontinental railway, and in just a century the grubby industrial waterfront of a tiny frontier town was transformed into the front steps of a major city. The First Narrows of Burrard Inlet, the narrow passage between Vancouver's Stanley Park and the North Shore, defines the entry to this city's exquisite natural harbour.

European settlers were lured here by the promise of land, wealth, and the seemingly unlimited potential of natural resources. Access to the rugged territory on either side of the harbour was originally provided by small boats, adequate to connect the isolated pioneer settlements and Native villages scattered around the Inlet. Several thousand new settlers lured by the promise of the railway, with their optimistic faith in the ideal of progress, saw few obstacles to their desire to develop, build and grow in this part of the New World. It was first predicted by George Grant Mackay, in 1890, that one day a bridge would join both sides of Burrard Inlet.

Mackay, one of the visionary breed who flocked to the Coast, was born in Inverness and lived all but the last five years of his life in the Scottish Highlands. He was intrigued by an exhibition of photographs and products from British Columbia at the 1883 Glasgow Exhibition, and in the summer of 1888, at the age of 62, he and his family moved to Vancouver. He was heavily involved in land speculation, and soon acquired 320 acres of prime land on the Capilano River in North Vancouver. By 1892 he had formed the Capilano Park Company, along with A.P. Horne and architect R. Mackay Fripp. They planned to develop their combined holdings of over 4,600 acres on the North Shore as recreational property. Mackay also spent time in the Okanagan, where he was known as *Gee-Gee*, and founded the towns of Benvoulin and Vernon. It was joked about in bars that when Mackay died, he would seize St. Peter by the lapel and say to him 'How are my chances for a townsite here?' Mackay's prophecies for Vancouver, made in a series of newspaper articles in 1890, were uncannily accurate. He foresaw not just the construction of a high level bridge at the First Narrows, but also a comprehensive electric streetcar system, and the development of exclusive residential areas on the North Shore. Mackay's genius was to see the potential for the entire region, and how it would be knit together by advanced technological systems, but he died in 1893, years before any of these events occurred.

Mackay's predictions were not isolated pipe dreams. By the end of the 19th century the public imagination had been inspired by countless heroic projects that were tying the continents together: enormous steam ships, stupendous bridges, and vast railway lines. Globe-spanning telegraph systems caused a revolution in communication, easily the equivalent of today's digital revolution involving computers and the Internet. Each successive technological achievement spawned more superlatives, and fuelled the competition to build the

George Grant Mackay

highest, the biggest and the greatest. The Brooklyn Bridge, which finally opened in 1883, after decades of conception and construction, was not only a milestone in the engineering of suspension bridges, but also provided the mechanism by which the separate boroughs of New York City could be amalgamated. Here was an object lesson for entrepreneurs in other cities. Progress, and its resultant prosperity, was accomplished through engineering and its technological landmarks. The builders of these great works were considered the heroes of their time, and were appropriately rewarded.

It was inevitable that this momentum of colonial settlement and exploitation of the New World would reach the Pacific Coast. Virtually unknown in Europe until the end of the 18th century, the area was home to Indian nations, who harvested the rich local resources. Seasonal fishing camps were situated around Burrard Inlet, known to the natives as Sasamat. English and Spanish explorers, seeking to reinforce their claim to the lands of Pacific North America, arrived in the area almost simultaneously. The Spaniards first identified the natural harbour at the mouth of the inlet, and called it the Brazo de Florida Blanca in honour of their Prime Minister. It was formally charted by Captain George Vancouver in June of 1792, who named it after Sir Harry Burrard, a former shipmate in the West Indies. European settlement of the area was slow, given the distance from other ports, the difficulty of access, and the ruggedness of the surrounding terrain. The region remained a quiet colonial backwater until Gold Rush fever in the mid-1850s lured thousands to the area. In 1859 the H.M.S. *Plumper*, under the command of Captain George H. Richards, was dispatched to survey Burrard Inlet for defensive purposes. Continuing growth led to more permanent settlements, and a transcontinental railway was promised—the price of British Columbia's admission to the new Canadian Confederation. Port Moody, located at the far eastern end of Burrard Inlet, was chosen as the terminus, and the first train arrived there in 1885. Even then, forces were already at work to extend the line an extra few miles to the struggling townsite of Granville, on the south side of the superb natural harbour located between the First and Second Narrows of the inlet. This turned out to be a visionary plan, and in 1887, only two years later, the first train pulled into the newly renamed City of Vancouver, popularly known as the Terminal City.

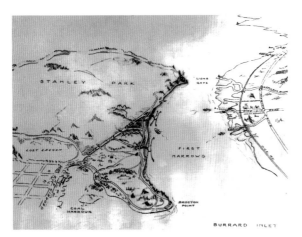

BURRARD INLET

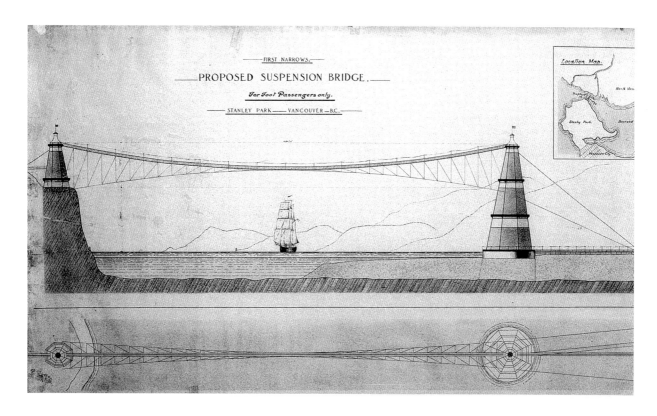

Calling this settlement a 'city' at the time was an act of wild optimism, as the entire town had burned to the ground the previous year. Feverish land speculation was already underway, with rapidly escalating prices and grandiose development schemes. The key player was the Canadian Pacific Railway, which had been given 5,800 acres in and around the old townsite to extend its rail line to Vancouver, land which it is still developing over a century later. In addition to prime waterfront parcels, the CPR was given much of the west side of Vancouver, later developed as the Kitsilano and Shaughnessy neighbourhoods. In a classic example of colonial imperialism, the native inhabitants were conveniently swept aside, squeezed onto reduced parcels of land with little economic value. Anything necessary for the growth of the city was simply taken as required.

Despite its importance, the natural harbour was the ultimate obstacle to metropolitan growth. The natural barriers of water and mountains isolated certain parts of the region, especially the highly desirable lands to the north. Indian Arm, an extended spur of the inlet, prevented access to these lands from the northeastern side. There were only two logical points at which Burrard Inlet could be crossed: the First Narrows, where the peninsula of Stanley Park reached within several thousand feet of the North Shore, and the Second Narrows, much farther to the east. For decades, the dream of spanning the harbour gave rise to countless speculative schemes and ventures, ranging from the crackpot to the grandiose.

Proposed suspension bridge for foot passengers, drawn by Engineer Fred L. Tytler in 1909.

In 1894, the Burrard Inlet Tunnel & Bridge Company received permission from the Federal government to construct, among other projects, a tunnel under the First Narrows. During the accelerating growth of the next few years both a tunnel and a bridge were seriously discussed. Population growth on the North Shore was explosive, and the City of North Vancouver, nicknamed *The Ambitious City*, was incorporated in 1907. By 1910 local boosters were speculating endlessly about the necessity of spanning the Narrows, raising the expectation that it was only a matter of time before it happened. The North Shore was one of the proposed sites for the new University of British Columbia, its chances predicated on the First Narrows being spanned. Regular ferry service began across the Inlet, and the future looked bright for new development. The imminent opening of the Panama Canal fuelled even more optimism, and enthusiasm for Vancouver's potential became unbounded. A fixed link between Vancouver and the North Shore seemed more likely than ever. West Vancouver, at the time a sleepy collection of summer cottages, was incorporated in 1912, and was anxious for a permanent link.

*WEST VANCOUVER NOW VERY ACTIVE*
*The members of the council recognize that the tunnel under the Narrows is of paramount importance and are working diligently with this end in view. The district of West Vancouver owns in the neighbourhood of $60,000 worth of the capital stock of the Vancouver Tunnel & Bridge Company.*
Vancouver Daily Province, April 20, 1912

These grandiose dreams died with the depression of 1913. Global economic forces conspired to end the Western boom as quickly and dramatically as it had begun. Plummeting commodity prices led to a combined collapse of local resource industries. The economy was devastated, and financial institutions collapsed one after another. On top of everything else, railway construction in the Fraser Canyon that year caused an enormous rock slide that blocked the salmon run and almost destroyed the lucrative canning industry. Speculative development schemes stalled, and the outbreak of the First World War in 1914 put an end to any hope for a quick recovery. Support for a harbour crossing evaporated, and the North Shore was destined to remain isolated for several more decades.

The Great War had spawned astounding technological advancements in aviation, shipbuilding, and other industries. Confidence in the future gradually returned, and the renewed global economy was hungry for raw materials. In the 1920s, Vancouver became Canada's Pacific gateway to booming world markets.

Political power in Canada was still centred in the east, and it took strong measures and strong voices to ensure consideration for western issues. As early as 1914, Member of Parliament and local booster Henry H. Stevens pushed for, and secured, the construction of Vancouver's first grain elevator, based on a reasonable assumption that the opening of the Panama Canal would ultimately make Vancouver the grain port of the future. Gerald Grattan McGeer, later the mayor of Vancouver, was a strong driving force behind local economic revitalization. Appointed as special counsel for B.C. in 1916, his persistent federal lobbying increased the westbound grain rates by ten percent, and brought a second grain elevator to Vancouver in 1923. McGeer was well connected; his wife Charlotte was a member of the wealthy Spencer merchant family, and a cousin to international entrepreneur A.J.T. Taylor, later the key figure in the emerging story of the bridge.

The drive towards regional expansion in the lower mainland of British Columbia was boosted by these new developments. Burrard Inlet was finally spanned with the opening of a low level bridge across the Second Narrows on November 7, 1925. This rickety structure used a series of trestle-piers and small spans to cross the inlet, with a Bascule counterweight that opened the centre span. Its tortuous approaches and two narrow lanes, split by a central railway track, contributed to make this an unreliable link, but despite these drawbacks its construction was hailed as the most important event in the history of the North Shore.

Returning prosperity was also evident on Vancouver's skyline. The first modern skyscrapers were seen, starting with the Medical Dental Building in 1928, followed closely by the Marine Building and the new headquarters for the Royal Bank. The landmark Hotel Vancouver, the third to bear the name, was begun. Just as Vancouver was once again booming, the Crash of 1929 shattered the world's economy. On October 24, Black Thursday, the market took a plunge that wiped out most small investors. Banks tried to shore up the market but by Monday businesses were collapsing like dominoes. The result was a full-on market free-fall on October 29, known as Black Tuesday. Buyers could not be found for stocks at any price, and the underpinnings of the global financial system collapsed. Wages plummeted, and countless thousands went bankrupt. Vancouver's progress was once more put on hold.

Yet for some, even these hard times held a glimmer of hope. As economies around the world struggled, the sudden availability of cheap skilled labour led to many public works projects, which had not seemed affordable in better times. Australia's landmark Sydney Harbour Bridge was completed in 1932. Hoover Dam, the world's largest, tamed the Colorado River in 1935. San Francisco's Golden Gate Bridge, talked about for many years, was finally opened in 1937; its 4,200 foot clear span was the longest in the world until 1959.

Hoover Dam

Second Narrows Bridge

A FUTURISTIC CONCEPTION OF VANCOUVER

Tourist · Shipping · Manufacturing · Lumber · Mining

Hard times notwithstanding, or perhaps because of them, there remained opportunities for entrepreneurs who could see them. Real estate, new or old, could be had for rock bottom prices, often for the value of unpaid property taxes, and those with cash prospered. Although Canada never had the enormous centralized public works programs seen in the United States, make-work projects were undertaken at the local level throughout the country. People readily accepted jobs whatever the rates and risks, and this newly available pool of cheap, seasoned workers mastered monumental tasks. In Vancouver, the Sea Island Airport and the Burrard Street Bridge were among the first projects to be finished. The new Vancouver City Hall, built near the geographic centre of the newly amalgamated city, was begun in 1935 and completed in time for the City's Jubilee the following year. The wooden structures at the Pacific National Exhibition were systematically replaced by a series of concrete Art Deco structures. St. James' Anglican Church replaced its aging wooden structure with a modernist concrete monument, designed by an English architect who had never visited the site. These isolated projects provided some relief and hope during a time when both were lacking for the huge numbers of people who remained unemployed.

Vancouver's greatest venture during the Depression was the construction of the Lions Gate Bridge. It was accomplished through the investment of private foreign capital fleeing British taxation, and realized chiefly through the determined efforts of one man, A.J.T. Taylor. He was well aware of the city's potential for growth, and knew that the local governments had no funds to build such a bridge. Taylor speculated that the bridge's construction could be financed by private sources, especially when labour costs were so low. The prize that would make this all worth while, the undeveloped lands in West Vancouver, lay within sight, and were available for the taking.

Taylor single-handedly attracted the necessary British capital that would make this project work. As economic conditions improved towards the mid-1930s, he faced unexpected political interference that delayed and threatened the project, and it took years to triumph over the forces of opposing vested interests. It was not until 1938 that the dream of a First Narrows crossing finally became a reality.

TAYLOR'S WAY

World Trade Routes Converge at Vancouver

THE FIRST NARROWS CROSSING occupies both a real and a symbolic place in Vancouver's history. The dream of linking the city with the mountains across Burrard Inlet had been as old as the city itself, yet the individual who achieved that connection, Alfred James Towle Taylor, remained an enigma in the public imagination. Despite his outgoing personality, his persona was deliberately modest. He spoke infrequently in public, and appeared rarely in official photographs. The press seldom mentioned his pivotal role, and he remained the man behind the scenes by choice, allowing others the full measure of glory that should rightfully have fallen upon him. The struggle to build the bridge took years, and materially affected his health, yet his achievements were hardly acknowledged, much less publicly commemorated. Not without a certain touch of irony, Taylor Way, the road that marks the entrance to the British Properties, remains his only memorial.

From early childhood until his death, Taylor was driven to extremes to achieve his visions. The son of a brilliant scientist whose gift of questioning Taylor inherited, and a nurturing mother, Alfred ('Fred') Taylor was born in Victoria, British Columbia on August 4, 1887. His father, George Taylor, employed by the British Museum as an entomologist, jumped at the chance to explore rare scientific finds in the western lands and waters of the New World. While in Victoria, George met and married Elizabeth Williams, the daughter of an Anglican minister. Affectionately called Bessie, she would give birth to four children, Fred, Ted, Willie and Helen. Unable to support his family with his scientific studies, George augmented his income by acting as a minister. Since neither pure science nor religion paid enough, he struggled to continue his research while carrying out his ministry. Bessie, devoted to her family, died at 38 giving birth to their fourth child. At great cost to himself and his children, George, before his death at the age of 57, would achieve his dream of establishing the Pacific Biological Station at Departure Bay, British Columbia, a scientific institution still operating today.

George Taylor pursued his passion for science more fervently following Bessie's death. Alone and unable to care for four young children, George had made plans to return to England, but at the last moment he was given a double parish on remote Gabriola Island that made it possible for him to remain. George's prolonged absences now forced his eldest son Fred, at the age of nine, into his mother's former role as family caregiver. Young Ted and younger Helen were under Fred's care, while Willie was with Bessie's parents in Victoria. In addition to being given the responsibility for household duties, Fred also had to care for his father's professional needs, constructing showcases for his specimens, and sharing a nine mile walk to church to play the organ during services. It was during those walks that Fred became close to his father, who was otherwise rarely home.

His father's absences and his mother's death inspired in Taylor a desire for knowledge which was both uncompromising and compensatory. Failure of an English Grammar examination ended his formal education at fourteen, and fuelled his determination to prove himself. An apprenticeship was secured for him at Dobeson's Foundries in Nanaimo. Small in build, *Little Hercules*, as he was known, worked from five in the morning to nine at night, and also ran an eight room boarding house, taking in and cooking for his co-workers. His interest in engineering had been sparked by conversations with his father and the study of his books on mechanics, and at sixteen it led him to apprentice with the Vancouver Ship Yards.

Fred's wages were meagre, and of the five dollars per month he earned, two were spent on the rent of a blackened CPR shack that he shared with contractor Frank Holt, prophetically, on the waterfront near the corner of Hastings and Burrard Streets. Within three years he had saved $119 to send to his father. He had gained a reputation of being the 'banner boy' among the apprentices, and in 1906 looked for a job that would give him further experience in engineering. Brilliant at his work, he moved up through the management of five different industrial companies in five years and established his first international contacts in engineering.

A job as inspector in the Mechanical Department of the General Electric Company took him briefly to Ontario. Returning to Vancouver, Fred took up residence at the exclusive men's Terminal City Club. One of

his new acquaintances was Duncan Drummond Young, just arrived from Scotland and working as sales manager of North Pacific Lumber. Young had two unmarried sisters back home, one of whom, Kathleen Mona, was deemed suitable for Fred, who initiated a year long correspondence. Recognizing the need for foreign industrial machinery in the booming economy of Western Canada, Fred and Duncan headed to Scotland in late 1911, in pursuit of financial backing to start their own company. Fred, who also had other, more personal pursuits on his mind, finally met Mona in person. They agreed they were compatible, and Mona made arrangements to move to Canada.

Rev. George William Taylor

Bessie Taylor

Fred at age four, with younger brother Ted.

24

Mona Young and Fred Taylor were married in Vancouver on June 25, 1912, just two months prior to George Taylor's death, and a few months after the opening of Taylor and Young Machinery Dealers in Vancouver. Taylor's way was to dream of bigger things, to play a big part in Vancouver's big business, but Duncan remained careful and conservative, frustrating Fred's initiative and daring. So, in 1913, Fred leapt at the opportunity of an all expense paid trip to Britain to learn about a new line of heavy machinery.

On the trip home a chance encounter changed Taylor's life. A fellow shipboard passenger gave him a copy of *Unto This Last* by John Ruskin, which defined business not by the question, 'How much do they make?' but by the answer to, 'To what purpose do they spend?' Ruskin's essays on political economy stressed that the acquisition of wealth was not the desired goal of business. This enlightened philosophy resonated with Taylor's own beliefs in the importance of personal integrity and philanthropy. From that moment on, and for the rest of his life, he carried and read and gave away copies of Ruskin's book.

On his way back across Canada, Taylor had, by fortuitous circumstance, also made a significant contact with the Imperial Oil Company, which was planning to build a major West Coast refinery. Impressed with the dynamic young Taylor, they hired his firm as local supervisors. This project was barely under way when war broke out in Europe, but the accelerated need for oil ensured its completion.

The war brought a number of changes to Taylor's life. Duncan signed up with the Highlanders and was sent to the Front, but Taylor was rejected for active service due to poor eyesight. Mona gave birth to Peter, their first son, and they moved to a house in the fashionable Jericho neighbourhood. In a pattern that was to become common to his life, Taylor proved adept at finding business opportunities during adverse times. As the local economy stagnated, Fred went south to San Francisco in search of a new, more highly polished image and further investment capital in a country not yet involved in the war. Having attained sufficient wealth to buy into the high-class Second Shaughnessy subdivision, Taylor found himself among rich friends. A garden of rare plants which had been collected by his father adorned his new place in the world.

The Ioco Refinery was one of the first large projects tackled by A.J.T. Taylor. On his way back from England in 1913, Taylor stopped in Toronto, and at a meeting of the Engineering Institute of Canada, made the contacts that led to his firm being chosen as local supervisors for the construction of a new refinery at Port Moody. They were ill-equipped to handle such a large project, but this opportunity presented an ideal reason to expand, and Taylor & Young Engineering was born. Construction began on the 100 acre site on July 29, 1914, and the plant came on stream in January 1915. A small townsite was located on the lower slope closer to the water, and a freight spur line connected the site to Port Moody. Taylor continued his involvement with the growing refinery throughout the war years, but also moved on to other large scale industrial projects.

**IOCO**

With Duncan overseas, the company was now under Fred's sole control, and he pursued industrial projects throughout British Columbia, including the development of company towns for mining interests. A key new employee was chartered accountant, John Anderson, who continued to work closely with Taylor right up to the completion of the Lions Gate Bridge. When Duncan Young returned from the war he became manager of a new company, the Taylor Mining Company, which allowed Fred the opportunity to diversify his own investments. This led to Taylor's first major setback.

In 1915 he had signed on to a mining venture with American investors who had staked claims for the Dolly Varden silver mine just east of the Alaska border. A narrow gauge railway had to be built to transport the ore, but by 1919, unforeseen problems with treacherous terrain had cost Taylor much more than he had estimated. The agreement for further funding was made verbally but the investors reneged, and Taylor was bankrupt. A sympathetic Creditors' Committee was set up, composed of business friends, and Taylor was appointed as chair. He salvaged his investment by acquiring controlling interest in the mine, and was ultimately able to complete the development. In the meantime his personal finances were in ruins.

Taylor lost the house in Shaughnessy, rendering the family temporarily homeless, but his financial and social recovery was remarkable. Family friends, the Chienes, provided the use of their lavish Point Grey home, which was later sold to the Taylors for a very friendly price. By 1922 Taylor had formed the Combustion Engineering Corp. Ltd., which held the Canadian rights to manufacture American-designed power plant equipment. In 1923, with his solvency secure and his expertise in internal combustion power needed in Toronto, Taylor moved his family east. There were now four children: Peter, Margaret, Kathleen and Joan. Duncan had decided to return to Britain. John Anderson accompanied Taylor east as secretary-treasurer. Just as family and business were being established in Toronto, an offer came from the Underfeed Stoker Company, England's most prominent combustion company, for Taylor to act as managing director. Taylor could not refuse, and rose in class and power overnight. Immediately, he became a member of the Board of International Combustion Corporation in London. An elegant home, *Glen Lodge*, set on three acres on prestigious Millionaires' Hill in St. George's District, twenty miles south of London, shot the Taylors right to the top of British society.

Duncan Young

Fred Taylor

Big business lurked in the manners and mansions of British high society in the twenties. The Taylor children were sent to high class boarding schools, while the unschooled Taylor was accepted on the face of his business reputation and self-schooled accent. Work, not school, brought his genius out. His lack of formal education did not prevent his membership in literary society. People, not books, taught him.

Taylor became a member of the Savage Club, founded in 1857 as a social club for men in literature and the fine arts. Early in its existence the Club expanded to include other intellectuals, such as men of science, though the bulk of the membership was still from the arts world. By 1882 the Club had 272 members and had achieved prominence in London, receiving its first of several honourary life members from the Royal family, the Prince of Wales, later King Edward VII. The regular event of the Club was the Saturday night house-dinners, often hosting illustrious guests, followed by entertainment by the members. Taylor was an active participant in these events, which expanded his contacts in the literary world. He became a friend of H.G. Wells. Frank Morley, a confidant who worked for the great London publishing house, Faber and Faber, based his 1952 book, *Dwelly Lane*, on Taylor.

His eyes fired with an abiding passion for bigger things, Taylor attracted everyone from the brightest wit to the dullest don. In contrast to the slow pace of English business, which one of his Swedish friends compared to 'swimming in tar,' Taylor cut an energetic figure in his new found high society. He enjoyed meeting young Rhodes Scholars, believing strongly in the schooling of boys, and having no plans except marriage for his daughters.

Taylor courted the best. Dinner with Lord Southborough was friendly and frequent. Southborough had served in many prominent appointments, including Civil Lord of the Admiralty during the Great War, and was privy to the inner sanctums of Buckingham Palace where King George VI sought his counsel and his company. He also acted as a representative of the Iveagh Trust, which handled part of the Guinness family fortune, and was conveniently familiar with Taylor's homeland, having visited Vancouver on business in 1908. Taylor's dream to dance in the midst of the royal classes had come true.

Mona Taylor, dressed for presentation at Court.

Britain in the 1920s was rich ground for big business and new ideas, which found their synthesis in discovering new ways for capital to flee British taxation by being diverted to investments in the colonies and elsewhere around the globe. Taylor's new friends could provide the investment power he needed to finance his transnational entrepreneurial plans. Britons of this time knew little and cared even less about the remote western lands of Canada, but Taylor understood their vast potential and was looking for the means to exploit it. In 1926 Taylor met the Honourable William Stephen Eyre, thirty years his senior, but with perfect qualifications for a partnership that would enrich both men for nine years. Eyre, an extremely wealthy retired banker, supplied the money to finance Taylor's dreams, which in turn gave Eyre a renewed purpose in life.

By 1928 Taylor felt that he had sufficient capital and investment in bank stocks to take care of his family, and began to plan for more speculative ventures. His sights were set on home, and he established a company, British Pacific Securities, to facilitate investment in British Columbia. Real estate in West Vancouver enticed the immediate triune investment of W.S. Eyre, the richest among them, Lord Southborough, and A.J.T. Taylor. Taylor's dream, to develop the 'empty lands' at the foot of the North Shore mountains, could only materialize if a fixed link was built to connect them to Vancouver. The 1929 Crash postponed those plans, as it radically altered the economic picture world wide. Taylor personally lost over half his holdings. The palatial mansion on Millionaires' Hill was let go, and a farm house in Rabbit Lane obtained, where two servants, who refused to leave, could barely be accommodated. Margaret's headmistress at Overstone Public Girls' School would not let her go and offered her a bursary to remain, and Peter continued on at Stowe.

Taylor again saw much opportunity in adversity. When times were tough, he shot for the moon. His grand vision for a bridge that would make West Vancouver accessible had to be achieved with private capital. If it were built during tough times, it could be accomplished for much less money, as labour and materials were cheap and readily available. The key was to first acquire possession of the undeveloped land in West

Vancouver. This land had been pre-empted by land speculators during the first boom of western settlement, but remained worthless, as the anticipated bridge or tunnel had not materialized. The speculators had stopped paying taxes, and vast amounts of property reverted to the municipality. Available for the cost of unpaid taxes, these lands were a powerful lure, and Taylor faced stiff competition. Other potential investors had already acquired interests in the lands, and were looking for backers. Taylor's advantage was his ready-made investment syndicate, bolstered by British tax laws which drove wealthy Britons to seek foreign investments. In 1930, Eyre insisted on a personal look at the potential investment, and he and Taylor made a trip to Vancouver that solidified their plans to proceed. On their way back to England, Taylor and Eyre stopped in Ottawa to confer with Prime Minister R.B. Bennett to determine if there was any opposition at the Federal level to a privately built bridge. To their surprise, Bennett expressed admiration for Taylor's plans to finance the bridge with private British funds and promised a remission of duty on materials. While Taylor was in his office, the Prime Minister also made telephone calls to secure cooperation from several government departments.

What loomed in Ottawa was not to be seen until much later. Even Taylor's visit to Edward Beatty, Chairman of the Canadian Pacific Railway, did not raise any alarm. Taylor was well aware of the CPR's previous opposition to a bridge, ostensibly due to potential navigation hazards, but in reality based on their resistance to any competition with their own land development schemes within the city of Vancouver. During their meeting Taylor presented Beatty with plans for the bridge, and to his surprise, Beatty did not appear antagonistic.

The trip had been worth it, and the bridge project looked like clear sailing. There was no obstruction in sight. Nothing should have stopped him.

THE BRIDGE GAME

BEFORE THE ONSET OF THE GREAT DEPRESSION, public opinion had been split over the necessity of a bridge across the First Narrows, and those who opposed the bridge displayed no shortage of arguments against it. Many decried the impact the causeway would have on Stanley Park, pronouncing its ruin. Others felt the bridge would be an unsightly imposition on the natural beauty of the harbour. The CPR alleged that the shipping lane was already too narrow, and that a bridge would endanger navigation and prevent any future widening of the Narrows. There was also the possibility of the bridge being bombed during wartime, closing the harbour and paralyzing the city. However, as the Depression dragged on, public opinion began to turn in favour of the bridge, and it came to symbolize new hope and a new start for Vancouver.

Moribund since 1914, the idea of a First Narrows crossing had been revived in 1924. West Vancouver Reeve David Morgan, inspired by a picture of the Clifton Suspension Bridge across the River Avon in England, persuaded the *Vancouver Daily Province* to run an artist's impression of a similar bridge across the Narrows. This conceptual scheme showed two 250 foot towers with a proposed span of 1,800 feet. It was through the publication of this image that the idea of a suspension bridge from Vancouver to the North Shore began to take hold.

In early 1926, James Ollason, West Vancouver's Municipal Clerk, offered two million dollars of tax land in exchange for the construction of a bridge. That spring, James A. Campbell, a prominent lawyer allied with the Liberal Party, was the first to begin serious negotiations about building a bridge at First Narrows. Campbell travelled East to seek financial backers, and the Dwight P. Robinson & Company, of Montreal and New York, offered $3,500,000 to back his plan. On June 7, Campbell began official talks with the City of Vancouver and the North Shore municipalities, but a competing plan surfaced at the same time. This second scheme was advanced by William Carey Ditmars of the Armstrong & Morrison Company, backed by contractors Stuart Cameron Limited, with a bridge designed by engineers Harrington, Howard and Ash of Kansas City. The Armstrong-Morrison proposal was for a 1,230 foot span with a maximum clearance of 165 feet and a road width of twenty-four feet. This would allow for 3,000 automobiles hourly, and if traffic increased, a twin bridge could be built alongside the first with the anticipated profits from the toll money.

In response to the competing applications, a Royal Commission was held, reporting back on January 15, 1927, that the construction of a bridge at First Narrows was technically feasible, although it recommended a span of 1,400 feet and a clearance of 190 feet. The province then issued two non-exclusive bridge charters, the Armstrong-Morrison Charter and the Campbell Charter.

Once provincial requirements had been met, the next issue for the potential developers was the acquisition of municipal permission to build an access road through Stanley Park. On June 25, 1927, a plebiscite was held, asking the citizens of Vancouver: 'Are you in favor of the construction of a Boulevard Roadway, without cost to the City, through a portion of Stanley Park to afford access to and from the proposed First Narrows Bridge, subject to a satisfactory agreement between the Board of Park Commissioners and the Bridge Company as to location and specifications?' The public remained sceptical of a First Narrows Crossing. With such a small population on the North Shore, and no reason for it to grow, this was seen by most people as a 'bridge to nowhere.' There was already a Second Narrows Bridge, and, it was felt, perfectly adequate local ferry service. The plebiscite was soundly defeated, and the bridge companies lost both their backing and their momentum.

The tax lands, however, still proved to be an irresistible lure to land speculators. Convinced of their value, H.H. Stevens stepped in and reserved several thousand acres of land in West Vancouver, north of Marine Drive and reaching to the 1,200 foot level. Stevens had been the single most influential individual in the development of the Port of Vancouver. Born in Bristol in 1878, his family had joined the mass migration to the colonies when he was twelve. By 1908, Stevens had established an accountant's and broker's office in Vancouver that had a wide variety of interests in timber, properties and industrial sites, but he also had interests in the public arena. By 1910 he was elected as a Vancouver Alderman, and the following year was elected MP for Vancouver Centre. While in public office, his mission was to develop Vancouver as a significant port, and Canada's window to the Orient. During the First World War he had False Creek dredged, and Granville Island was established as an industrial enclave. He agitated for western shipyards to receive contracts, and when access to the harbour for larger ships became an issue, had the First Narrows dredged from a width of 400 feet to 1,600 feet.

Stevens had received his financial backing in the West Vancouver land deal from a wealthy Scot living in Tacoma, Washington, who died suddenly in 1929. Vancouver was starting to feel the effects of the Depression, and Stevens could not find any new backers. No local businessman would invest in the lands

H.H. Stevens

Looking south on Burrard Street from the Marine Building, 1931.
The Hotel Vancouver stood unfinished for ten years during the Depression.

without the certainty of a bridge. In a chance encounter with A.J.T. Taylor, Stevens explained his predicament. Taylor could not believe his luck, as he was considering just such a deal himself. Seizing the competitive opportunity, Taylor initiated negotiations with West Vancouver on behalf of his British investors.

Other events were in motion that would drastically alter the situation. Their futures uncertain, the two firms that had been granted bridge charters merged on June 17, 1930, under the name First Narrows Bridge Company Limited. W.C. Ditmars, known as Vancouver's major bridge builder, was now President of the company. Ditmars had been involved in the construction of the first bridge across the Fraser River at New Westminster, and enjoyed recalling that as early as 1911 he had discussed with engineers the possibility of bridging the First Narrows.

Then, on September 19, 1930, a dramatic shipping accident knocked out the Second Narrows Bridge, stranding hundreds of cars on the wrong side. This event threw the District of North Vancouver into receivership, leaving no public resources available to repair the bridge, which sat unusable for the next four years. More than any other event, this disaster helped silence public opposition to the idea of a privately financed First Narrows crossing. In January of 1931, Ditmars contacted Taylor in London to inquire if his syndicate was interested in investing in the bridge project. This fit well with Taylor's plans, but to avoid any hint of political favouritism he was determined to buy the existing charters rather than seek a new one.

The amount of capital Taylor required to build the bridge and to develop the land was staggering. Eyre's money alone could not begin to cover what was required, so Taylor's long time friend and supporter, Lord Southborough, brought this ambitious scheme to the attention of the Guinness interests, and two of their representatives made a trip to West Vancouver to view the site. Mr. Greenwood, a lawyer, and C.H. Bland, a financial advisor, sailed from England with Taylor on May 27, 1931, to tour the proposed ventures in West Vancouver. When they arrived, the party was joined by Joseph B. Leyland, Reeve of West Vancouver, who accompanied them on their visit to the tax lands. Leyland, anxious to impress, brought two enormous picnic baskets. They stopped at the top of 15th Street, which ended in wilderness at Mathers Avenue. It was a clear, warm June day, and Leyland later recalled feeling like Moses on the Mountain. After lunch, the party left, captivated by the panoramic view and the enormous potential for development.

The deal for the land was struck between West Vancouver and the British capitalists. For over 4,000 acres, the municipality would receive a grand total of $75,000 in cash, paid over four years. In exchange, the developers would spend a million dollars on improvements, including a golf course, roads, water lines, sewers and a school site. West Vancouver residents were to be employed to do the work. A plebiscite was held in West Vancouver on the deal; 1,329 voted for, and 26 against. This decision saved the municipality from almost certain bankruptcy. Although West Vancouver had committed over 4,000 acres to the project, they realized when they studied their maps that the municipality was about 1,000 acres short. Reeve Leyland hurried to Victoria to acquire enough Crown land to make up the difference.

By the time Taylor returned to Vancouver in October of that year, a series of companies had been formed in England to carry out his investment schemes. British Pacific Properties Ltd., a subsidiary of the investment syndicate, was formed specifically to develop the 'Highlands' on West Vancouver's Upper Levels. On December 4, controlling interest was acquired in the First Narrows Bridge Company, and in addition to the existing charters they inherited the services of Monsarrat & Pratley of Montreal, the leading bridge design firm in Canada. Everything was now in place for Taylor's scheme, and municipal and provincial approvals were considered somewhat of a formality. The last hurdle was Federal permission under the *Navigable Waters Act*, and Taylor's proposal considerably exceeded the requirements of the existing bridge charters they had just acquired.

Although Taylor now had all the technical aspects under control, he had not foreseen the political battles which were to delay the project for years. While he was fighting those battles, Taylor embarked on many other projects abroad. He continued to promote British Columbia at every opportunity, calling it the 'last great empire for adventure,' but sought to diversify his investments wherever he could.

*Partly because of the association of its name and its location, also its largely Anglo-Saxon population, and the fact that it was last to join Confederation, British Columbia presents to the average British mind a province distinct from the rest of Canada, said A.J.T. Taylor of London, England this morning.*
Vancouver Daily Province, June 14, 1932

Over these years, Taylor and his backers amassed great wealth. In the midst of the global depression, they continued to find huge investment opportunities. British Pacific Securities had not been able to keep pace with the partners' plans for expansion. The British Pacific Trust was established, with the shareholders being given the first chance to invest in any 'sure things.' In just one of their bold moves, Taylor's syndicate signed a long-term lease on the British Empire Building in New York, to be built as part of the Rockefeller Center. In addition to land speculation and development, Taylor sought to invest in new technology, and agreed to take on the world rights to Buckminster Fuller's Dymaxion car. Another project that took years to accomplish was the construction of the Earl's Court Exhibition Building in London, at the time reputedly the largest exhibition centre in the world. While for many the 1930s continued to be their worst time economically, Taylor's ambition, vision and luck were unlimited.

Planning was already underway on this monumental development in Midtown Manhattan by the time of the 1929 Crash. Originally conceived as a philanthropic venture that would provide a new home for the Metropolitan Opera, by February, 1932, its focus changed to that of a purely commercial venture, renamed as Rockefeller Center, after its major developers. A landmark tower for the RCA Corporation was the focal point of this sophisticated urban ensemble. The lower structures facing prestigious Fifth Avenue were designed as centres of international trade, and two were reserved for French and British interests. The promenade between them, which led on axis to the front door of the RCA Building, became known as the Channel Gardens, since it, like the English Channel, separated France *(La Maison Française)* to the south from the United Kingdom (the British Empire Building) to the north. British Pacific Securities agreed to lease the British Empire Building, and on July 2, 1932, Lord Southborough, as head of the syndicate, laid the cornerstone at an elaborate ceremony. Prominent members of the English nobility, as well as diplomatic and consular representatives from around the world, attended, and the Hon. H.H. Stevens, Canadian Minister of Trade and Commerce, spoke. Taylor and Eyre were also present at the ceremony, which was broadcast on radio nation-wide by the National Broadcasting Company. The building opened in early June of the following year. Taylor maintained his contacts with John D. Rockefeller Jr., and together they explored other ventures, including the possibility of a National Theatre in London.

# ROCKEFELLER CENTER

Above: Lord Southborough laying the cornerstone of the British Empire Building July 2, 1932.

Right: Rockefeller Centre. The Associated Architects: Reinhard & Hofmeister; Corbett, Harrison & MacMurray; Raymond Hood, Godley & Fouilhoux.

While working on the deal that would lead to the construction of the Lions Gate Bridge, Taylor was simultaneously working on an enormous project in London. A company was formed under the auspices of the British Pacific Trust to finance the construction of the Earl's Court Exhibition Building. The proposed structure required nearly twenty acres, and was the only available site in Central London big enough. Taylor had 'a hell of a time' assembling the required properties. The design of the complex was finally started in 1935 by C. Howard Crane, an American who maintained practices in London and Detroit, and was the acclaimed architect of the Music Box and the Theatre Guild Theatre in New York. At the time of its completion in 1938 this was reported to be the largest exhibition centre in the world. Cutting-edge technology was employed to make the vast interior spaces flexible. In just one hour the floor of the Main Hall could be hydraulically lowered, and flooded to form a gigantic swimming pool holding 2.25 million gallons of water. The Exhibition Building is still in active use today, and when its seating is in place it is still the largest covered auditorium in Europe.

# EARL'S COURT

Fred Taylor's business activities coincided briefly with those of Buckminster Fuller, one of the greatest engineers, designers and futurists of the twentieth century. Cars were Fred's lifelong hobby, and when he was in New York in July of 1932, for the laying of the cornerstone of the British Empire Building, Taylor slipped out to the Automobile Show, where he first saw Fuller's ideas for a radical new car design. When Fred returned to New York the following summer for the building's opening, he heard again about this new car and pursued the idea of investing in its production.

Buckminster Fuller had created a fair amount of international publicity in the late 1920s for his Dymaxion House design, an innovative concept for a mass-produced, self-sustaining, hexagonal house, hung from a central mast. It could be erected anywhere that it could be transported. 'Dymaxion' was a contraction of the words 'DYnamic', 'MAXimum', and 'IONs'—three words Fuller used often in his speeches. The next step in Fuller's concept of decentralized housing was the development of a 'flying car', the 'Dymaxion Omni-directional Human Transport,' that would allow unlimited access to these houses. The jet technology required to make the car fly had not yet been developed, so Fuller threw his energy into developing a proto-

type car, based on then available airplane technology.

By the summer of 1933 Fuller had teamed up with Starling Burgess, an engineer and famed yacht designer, and established a factory at Bridgeport, Connecticut where they built the first full-size Dymaxion Car prototype. It was a streamlined, aluminum bodied, three-wheeled car, which Fuller always intended as the first step in building an automobile that could fly. Others, including Taylor, became interested in the commercial applications if it was developed only as land transport. The idea of a sleek new car was extremely seductive, given the public interest in the streamline style and the desperate straits of the automobile industry. Taylor was taken to Bridgeport to see the

prototype, and agreed to take on the world rights to the car. Colonel William Francis Forbes-Semphill, a British aviation expert, was sent over on the *Graf Zeppelin* in 1933 to test the car's performance. On one of these practice runs, Semphill was involved in a high-speed collision with a conventional car at the entrance to the Chicago World's Fair. The driver of the other car was killed, and Semphill was badly injured. The unfavourable publicity about this fatal accident scared off the English investors, and contributed to the closure of Fuller's factory the following year. Only three prototypes of the car were ever built, the second of which has survived. Fuller and Taylor remained in contact over the years, and last met at Taylor's Washington apartment in 1943.

# THE DYMAXION CAR

Starling Burgess and Buckminster Fuller in front of the first Dymaxion car, July 21, 1933.

W. H. HILLIER

The Marine Building is the architectural gem of Vancouver, conceived as a central location for those involved in the shipping trades and port activities of the city. The increasingly prosperous years that followed the First World War were fuelled by the success of the Port of Vancouver. In 1929, construction began on the tallest and most prestigious office building in the city. Stimsons Canadian Development Co., a subsidiary of a Toronto company, planned The Marine Building as the most lavish address in the city. It represented the height of the Art Deco movement in Western Canada. Architects McCarter & Nairne described their masterwork as 'some great sea crag rising from the sea, clinging with sea flora and fauna, tinted in sea-green, touched with gold.'

Marine motifs run riot throughout the building's exterior and interior ornamentation. The lobby entrance is a grand portal that symbolizes the city's role as a gateway to the Orient. The abstracted sun's rays, against which Canada Geese fly into the sunset, were originally covered with gold leaf. The cathedral-like splendour of the lobby is illuminated by stained glass panels at each end that echo the sunrise and sunset. Subdued indirect lighting shines upward from ship's prows surging forward from the wall surfaces. Cast brass elevator doors are a riot of geometric ornament, and the interiors of the elevator cabs are superb examples of inlaid marquetry, using a dozen different kinds of wood. The lobby's

ornate cast plaster ceiling was originally painted in vibrant blues, reds and greens and highlighted with gold leaf.

The developers' timing could not have been worse. They had spent twice the original budget, a total of $2.5 million, and the onset of the Depression bankrupted them. The Marine Building was repossessed by its American financiers, and was offered to the city for one million dollars for use as a City Hall, but this bargain was declined. Fred Taylor saw it as the ideal flagship for the British Pacific ventures in Vancouver, with the First Narrows and the North Shore mountain slopes highly visible from its harbour-side windows. By July, 1933, he had acquired this landmark for less than a million dollars.

# THE MARINE BUILDING

Architects rendering of the Marine Building, 1928.

The Marine Building Lobby, September. 29, 1930.

Throughout the years of expanding his global investments, Taylor's planning for the First Narrows bridge continued, although it was taking longer than he expected. By April 13, 1933, the Provincial government had approved its construction, based on Taylor's acquisition of the existing charters. From April to November Taylor continued his negotiations with Vancouver City Council and the Board of Park Commissioners. At this point a fierce battle broke out over the technical requirements of the bridge. The Chairman of the CPR, the recently knighted Sir Edward Beatty, called publicly for the 'widest possible span' for the navigable channel. Vancouver City Council, looking for the Bridge Company to provide further infrastructure improvements, rejected their first proposal. Taylor, anxious to proceed, was ready to accede to what he felt were unreasonable demands. On August 18, the City of North Vancouver agreed to the bridge, followed shortly afterwards by the Districts of North and West Vancouver. On August 19 the Vancouver Parks Board approved the principle of a bridge, insofar as it would affect Stanley Park. Taylor attended the Vancouver Council meeting on November 9, 1933, which dissolved into fractious name-calling, accusations of collusion and political interference, and constant interruptions. Every one of the Aldermen had instantly become an expert on technical details. Mayor Louis D. Taylor (no relation to Fred) seemed strongly in favour of the proposal, but was unable to maintain control of the proceedings.

*We must not be narrow-minded. In five years' time West Vancouver may be part of the city.*

Mayor Louis D. Taylor, quoted in the *Vancouver Daily Province*, April 13, 1933

The local newspapers were having a field day with the issue. The *Vancouver Daily Province* consistently railed against the proposed First Narrows Bridge. Vancouver Mayor L.D. Taylor alleged that the newspaper opposed the project because it was owned by Southam, which in turn had the exclusive contract for the CPR's printing.

Recognizing the impossibility of the situation, Taylor telephoned the mayor later that night, proposing a plebiscite on the issue, to be held at his Company's expense. He was out on a limb, as he had had no time to contact London to let them know what he was doing. City Council, mollified by the Company's offer to pay the expenses, agreed the next day to the plebiscite. This started the public debate all over again. The same contentious issues were again dragged through the newspapers, but this time the Company was more prepared to deal with them. They had already allowed for an increase in the size of the span, and were also able to prove that most of the seemingly unrelated objections were being fuelled by spokesmen tied to the CPR.

# THE EXPERT DECIDING IT

*Opponents of the bridge desire an 1,800 foot span. The position of the CPR is equally consistent throughout. The railway company does not want any kind of a bridge at the First Narrows.*

*Vancouver Daily Province,*
June 5, 1934

*The intrigue, the journalistic machinations, the kite-flying and the stealthy innuendoes that have centred about this structure ever since it was first proposed constitute the most offensive and preposterous affront that has been offered to any self-contained community since the Babylonians came down and enslaved Jerusalem. In all history there is recounted no more insidious attempt to flout the public will and debauch public opinion than has been apparent in the series of attacks launched against everything and everybody connected with this project.*

*Vancouver Sun,* September 6, 1934, blaming the *Daily Province* for delays in the approval of the First Narrows Bridge

Editorial cartoon from the *Vancouver Sun*, September 29, 1933.
St. James Street was the national headquarters of the CPR.

Plans for the bridge were forwarded to the Vancouver Town Planning Commission on November 20, 1933. On December 11, they issued their opinion, narrowly passed by five votes to four, expressing opposition to the bridge, calling it premature and inadequate in design. One of the votes against the bridge was cast by G.L. Thornton Sharp, partner in the firm Sharp & Thompson, architectural consultants for the recently completed Burrard Street Bridge. The Commission pointed out that the clearance of 200 feet would bar certain ships from entering Vancouver's harbour, but that San Francisco would still be available to them, as the Golden Gate Bridge would have a 220 feet clearance. The Commission expressed concern with the deteriorated local economy, and advised against any measures which would disperse the population, which still had vacant, undeveloped land, much of which was owned by the CPR.

Surprisingly the Commission had no problems with the impact of the bridge on Stanley Park. They noted the advantage of a firebreak through the centre of the park, and the causeway fit in with their ideas for new public amenities. Sharp & Thompson were busy preparing plans for several grand projects in and around the park, including a bathing pavilion on English Bay, and an extensive museum complex. But the Town Planning Commission was completely out of touch with the citizens of Vancouver. The lack of access to the North Shore, and the desperate need for employment had finally turned the tide of public opinion. On December 13, the plebiscite passed handily in all wards, with 17,000 out of 24,000 voting in favour of the bridge.

In the spring of 1934, Taylor renewed his efforts to seek further investment in the British Pacific Trust. Bryan Walter Guinness, the son of the First Lord Moyne, was already a Director, and the possibility was open that the Guinness family would be able to provide further funding. The Guinnesses had an earlier, indirect connection with the West Coast. John Ross Mahon, from a landed family in County Galway, had been in partnership with one branch of the family as Guinness Mahon. They had established a number of offices including in Dublin, London, and Ahascragh, Ireland, where the Mahon family had its estate, *Castlegar*. Mahon had no children, and chose his favourite nephew, John Fitzgerald Mahon, to run the Ahascragh office. John's younger brothers, Edward and Gilbert, had moved to British Columbia around 1889. They had been involved in mining in the Kootenays, and had established a camp that grew into the town of Castlegar, named after their family estate. On a trip to visit them, John became convinced that Vancouver, the only British port of consequence on the West Coast, was destined to become a great metropolis, and ultimately Britain's gateway to the Orient. The Mahons established the North Vancouver Land & Improvement Company, which successfully developed much of the City of North Vancouver. This was not the first or last time that British investment had successfully been brought into the region.

46

G.L. Thornton Sharp

West Vancouver Reeve and Council signing the First Narrows Bridge Agreement, May 12, 1934.
Left to right: James Duncan, Municipal Engineer; Councillor Lance Garthorne; Councillor William Dickinson; John Anderson,
British Pacific Properties; Solicitor Ronald P. Stockton, British Pacific Properties (standing); Reeve Joseph B. Leyland; R. Gordon
Robson, Municipal Solicitor (standing); William Herrin, Municipal Clerk; Councilor Robert Fiddes; Councillor Gerald D. Elgar.

The party of 'distinguished financiers' arrived by private rail car. From left, A.J.T. Taylor, Managing Director of British Pacific Trust; Lord Southborough, Director of the Trust and head of the party; Bryan Walter Guinness, the son of Lord Moyne and also a Director; Viscount Elveden (Arthur Guinness, the son of Rupert Cecil Guinness, the Second Earl of Iveagh); J. Fyfe Smith, B.C. Director of Canadian National Railways and Chairman of the Vancouver Parks Board, who was welcoming the party; C.H. Bland, a trustee of the Iveagh Trust; and W.S. Eyre, of Grace & Company, London bankers.

*Vancouver Sun,* June 7, 1934

*Taylor, who had the benign, precise mien of a country schoolteacher, moved in with his plan and a fine flair for the dramatic. When the first party of Guinnesses and advisors came to Canada, he saw to it that a private railway car carried them across the country. On the arrival of the party he whisked them to the exclusive Vancouver Club for a lunch of fresh-caught B.C. salmon, poured his guests some imported Irish whisky (none of the Guinnesses drank stout), and then led them to the rear of the club where the windows look out across the harbour to the Lions' Gate and the mountain he was asking them to buy. It was a nicely timed unveiling and the party was entranced.*

The Guinness family is possibly the greatest success story in the history of British business. Their empire was founded though the efforts of Arthur Guinness, a Protestant Irishman born in 1725. Arthur rented his first brewery outside of Dublin in 1756, but his output was small compared to that of his many rivals. In 1761 he married Olivia Whitmore, a Dublin heiress, which allowed him to expand his derelict brewery into what eventually became the single biggest business enterprise in Ireland. He fathered 21 children, ten of whom survived, starting a dynasty that through its many branches has control of business interests around the world. Over several hundred years the family, through a calculated series of advantageous investments and marriages, established itself as one of the most important lineages in Britain.

Once financially successful, the Guinnesses took steps to formally establish a noble pedigree for themselves. As early as 1781 Arthur

and his brothers appropriated without authority the coat of arms of the venerable Magennis family of County Down, one of the oldest and most powerful of the Irish clans. The family continued to exploit this tenuous connection, when Edward Cecil Guinness was created Baron Iveagh of County Down, a title given 268 years earlier to one Sir Arthur Magennis by James I of England. As there is no evidence that the family had roots in County Down or any relations with the Magennis clan, Edward appears to have chosen the title 'Iveagh' to help legitimize the appearance of inherited nobility. The buying of titles through political contributions was an open secret, and Prime Minister Lloyd George observed 'it is a far cleaner method of filling the party chest than the methods used in the United States.'

Rupert Guinness, the Second Lord Iveagh, made his first trip to Vancouver in 1917, when he was recruiting for the Royal Navy. His

next visit was in September, 1949, the first time he had a chance to see the bridge and suburbs he had helped create. Guinness, considered one of the ten richest men in the world, continued to invest in Vancouver, including in the development of Park Royal Shopping Centre, on Squamish Band land at the west approaches to the bridge.

The Guinness family interests in Vancouver were divided in the 1950s. The Moyne branch retained British Pacific Properties Ltd. Of the more than 4,000 acres acquired by the company, only 1,600 have been developed, leaving a vast and very valuable asset. Family members the Marquis of Normanby and the Hon. Finn Guinness currently sit on the company's Board of Directors. The Iveagh side of the family retained the bridge, Park Royal and the Marine Building, but has since sold them and diversified its assets.

# THE GUINNESS FAMILY

The jewel in the crown of the British Properties was a spectacular golf course laid out over the difficult sloping terrain. Extensive grading and planting was required to make the design, by golf course architect Stanley F. Thomson of Toronto, work properly. The course was opened in 1937, after four years of planning and construction. The sprawling clubhouse was designed by J.F. Dawson of Olmsted Brothers, with Palmer & Bow as supervising architects. Although completed in 1938, the clubhouse was not officially opened until May 17, 1939.

# BRITISH PROPERTIES

Map of 'The Highlands,' July 1935. Many of the streets were named after directors and investors in British Pacific Properties.

*It's nice to have the work, but they sure as hell shouldn't have sold them near as much land as they did.*
Frank Colpitts, one of the loggers hired to clear the British Properties

By 1932, land was being cleared for this new residential development, then known as the 'Highlands.' At the time, this was the only major real estate development under way in Canada. No expense was spared in making this the most desirable residential location in and around Vancouver. Large amounts of investment capital were required to prepare the land, which was essentially wilderness. The Olmsted Brothers, based in Brookline, Massachusetts, were hired to prepare a plan for the subdivision. This prominent firm was the successor to that established by Frederick Law Olmsted, preeminent American landscape architect of the nineteenth century and the designer of New York's Central Park. By 1937 construction work, including grading, road paving and the provision of services, had cost about $1,500,000. The original subdivision comprised only a fraction of the lands that British Pacific Properties had acquired, and provided about 450 lots with an average size of 1 ¼ acres. The registered name of Capilano Estates never caught on, and it was popularly called the British Properties, after the company. The exclusive ethnic nature of this enclave was protected by the Company's restrictions against ownership. Persons of Asiatic or African descent, other than servants, could not reside here, and although racial restrictions are not enforced, they remain in place today. Almost no lots were sold before the onset of the Second World War effectively put the project on hold. After the war the lots were re-subdivided to smaller sizes, the trees were logged off to highlight the spectacular views, and postwar growth ensured the success of this 'Suburb in the Sky.'

Photograph taken at the 'Capilano Estates' section of the British Properties
Back Row standing: James F. Dawson, Landscape Architect of Olmsted Bros., of Brookline, Mass.; Stanley F. Thompson, Golf Course Architect, Toronto.
Front Row left to right: John Anderson, Secretary-Treasurer; A.J.T. Taylor, President and Engineer-in-Chief, British Pacific Properties Ltd.; G.S. Conway, Construction Engineer of the project. Circa 1935.

Through Lord Southborough's prompting, Rupert Guinness, the second Earl of Iveagh, and his two brothers Arthur Ernest Guinness and Walter Edward, the First Lord Moyne, agreed to invest the major share of money necessary to finance Taylor's schemes in West Vancouver.

The sudden death of W.S. Eyre in August, 1935 was a huge loss to Taylor, both personally and financially, and increased the urgency of the situation. Despite previous assurances from Prime Minister R.B. Bennett, vested political interests continued to block Federal approval of the bridge proposal.

Business acquaintances warned Taylor that this delay was due to the Company's lack of lobbying in the House, and their refusal to contribute to Party funds. Horrified by these realities, he decided to wait until after the next election to press for final approval. He spent his time assuring the financing of the bridge, and promoting the benefits that would accrue to the City from it. At a time of economic doldrums, the possibility of such a construction project was becoming increasingly attractive, and Vancouver Council sent the City Solicitor to Ottawa to appear before a Special Committee set up by the Department of Public Works. Further delays ensued, including those created by public statements by the Prime Minister, who suddenly developed an opinion that the span was not wide

*Dear Leyland,*

*The only disappointment we have had from the entire development has been the attitude of Ottawa on the First Narrows Bridge, and as I have already told you privately, it has been absolutely inexplicable how any administration in Canada could have delayed a great public work like the Bridge during a period when work of any sort was so urgently needed.*

A.J.T. Taylor to Reeve Leyland, August 15, 1935

enough, and that it should be increased to 1,800 feet, but refused to name the authority on whom he had based this opinion.

Taylor was incredulous at these latest developments. The citizens of Vancouver had approved the bridge, and the provincial government had already accepted the company's calculations of the bridge's necessary span. In frustration, Taylor travelled to Ottawa to meet again with Bennett. The tone of the meeting verged on the belligerent. Taylor repeated the acceptance of the proposed span of 1,500 feet. Bennett reiterated his desire to see a span of 1,800 feet, despite his unwillingness to say why. To Bennett's annoyance, Hugh Stewart, the Minister of Public Works, confirmed that the width of the channel at high tide was 1,650 feet, and the

52

navigable channel only 950 feet. After further heated exchanges of opinion, Bennett intoned 'This may be so, but all I want, Mr. Taylor, is a bridge adequate for all time—adequate for the unborn children of Canada, whose custodian I am.'

The background influence of the CPR was obvious, but Bennett deflected Taylor's accusations of its interference. After further heated debate, Bennett declared that the long meeting was over. It was obvious that the Prime Minister's objections had no basis in the engineering of the proposed bridge. Stewart invited Taylor to come to his office later, and after hesitant discussion, a suggestion was made that if the South Pier could be moved north 50 feet, and the North Pier were moved north 100 feet, the span would be increased to 1,550 feet, and that this might be an acceptable compromise. Taylor agreed instantly, although it was unlikely that much could be accomplished before the next election, rumoured to be imminent.

Taylor now returned to his efforts at finding allies for his venture. He had appealed in 1933 to the British Government to fund the bridge under the Lord Milner Plan that supported home industries; they had agreed, but only if British steel was used. This proved to be impractical, so Taylor looked for suppliers closer to home. At the time, there were only two companies with branches in Vancouver that could build the bridge, the Dominion Bridge Company, and the Hamilton Bridge Company, whose subsidiary the Western Bridge Company was owned by Colonel Victor Spencer, Taylor's second cousin, and Frank Ross, later Lieutenant Governor of British Columbia. Taylor confided some of his problems to Ross, who suggested that the two steel companies take shares in the project, and split the work. Ultimately the Western Bridge Company invested $750,000 in the project, and Dominion Bridge invested $500,000, a move which certainly impressed Taylor's English backers.

*BENNETT'S 'PRIVATE BLOCKADE'*
*The First Narrows Bridge promoters today received official notification of the Government's latest move to block the First Narrows Bridge project... The blockade is the Prime Minister's own private opposition, for some reason undisclosed but guessed at... The Prime Minister's opposition may wreck the project.*
*Vancouver Sun*, September 10, 1934

Finally, in late 1935, events seemed to turn in Taylor's favour. Bennett's Conservative government was by now widely perceived as corrupt, and on October 23, they were decisively defeated. William Lyon Mackenzie King and the Liberal party were to form the new government. Taylor had resisted all efforts to politicize the issue, and had refused to make any political donations—he was thus perceived as 'clean', and above sordid political partisanship. Ian MacKenzie, a pro-bridge Liberal, one of the Members elected for Vancouver, was appointed Minister of National Defence. After a brief period to allow the new government to settle in, Taylor began a new round of negotiations. On Taylor's return to Canada on December 3, he was astounded to receive a letter from his long-time associate John Anderson, explaining what had happened the previous week in Ottawa. He was having lunch with Major Moodie, an organizer for the Liberal Party, at a local restaurant. Anderson had visited the men's washroom, and found a briefcase in one of the cubicles. Taking it back to the table, Anderson and Moodie agreed to contact a lawyer, and opened the case in his presence. The first letters they extracted contained a description of a plot to use Members of Parliament to delay permission to build the bridge until the Bridge Company agreed to certain conditions. Further intrigues were detailed in other papers in the case. Uncertain what to do, the three men copied the letters. Within twenty-four hours Anderson had received threats against his life, and spent several days under RCMP protection.

These letters were shown to MacKenzie King and other officials. Despite some incredulity about the way the letters were found, there was great concern over the implication of a political scandal, but still there was no movement on approval of the bridge. Frustrated to the point of distraction, Taylor finally achieved a meeting with King on February 27, 1936. He carried to this meeting a letter of introduction from Lord Southborough, who knew King well. Over the next few weeks there was a constant stream of letters and cables between King, Southborough and Taylor, whose greatest concern now was to gain the fastest possible approval in order to begin construction of the causeway. Due to the fire hazard from clearing of brush and blasting, the trees in Stanley Park had to be cleared before the end of May, or another year's delay would ensue.

Mayor Gerry McGeer

Taylor was confined to his hotel room by a diagnosis of threatened pneumonia. Lying awake, he decided to enlist as many local allies as possible. Mustering his determination after midnight, he placed a call to Gerald Grattan McGeer, Mayor of Vancouver and Liberal Member of Parliament, and related by marriage to his second cousin. McGeer was known as a fiery orator, passionate in his views, and a political scrapper. A large part of his career had been spent battling the CPR, arguing fiercely for the relief of restrictive freight rates that discriminated against western ports. In his first term as mayor, McGeer was fervently promoting make-work projects, including a new City Hall that would be ready in time for Vancouver's Jubilee in 1936. A strong proponent of the First Narrows Bridge, he was pushing to have it started in time for his Jubilee celebrations.

McGeer came to Taylor's hotel the next day, and agreed to re-open the debate in Parliament. It was going to be Vancouver versus Ottawa—why would the Federal Government not let the citizens have what they wanted? On March 24, McGeer raised the issue in the House, with King's foreknowledge, just before adjournment. McGeer took a firm stand that the City of Vancouver wanted a bridge, no matter who paid for it, and that if the Dominion Government scared off the English backers with its continued and inexplicable delays, then perhaps they should pay for it themselves.

King was getting the message from all directions, but Federal assurances of action were still vague. It would be politically destructive to the Liberal Government if the bridge were not approved, but no reason could be given for the delay. Taylor knew that his next step was to withdraw the proposal, and he was prepared to do so. He knew how this would play out in public opinion. Two and one-half years after the proposal was first made, the Federal Government was still withholding approval for a project over which it had little jurisdiction. Taylor's final tactic was to indicate that his contacts would ensure a public inquiry, which neither King, the new Prime Minister, nor Bennett, now the Leader of the Opposition, wanted to face. Exhausted, Taylor retreated to England.

There were no cards left to play in the bridge game. On April 29, 1936, an Order-in-Council finally provided Federal assent. For Vancouver, at least, the grim years of the Depression seemed over, and the long anticipated work on the First Narrows crossing could now begin. Vancouver's Golden Jubilee Year held great promise; McGeer could not only boast of the new City Hall being built, but also a fine new bridge, the longest span in the British Empire. His repeated suggestions to call it the 'Jubilee Bridge' were politely rebuffed by the bridge company. The bridge remained unnamed until October 26, 1937, when the official announcement declared that it would be called Lions Gate.

Vancouver City Hall

*You have delighted me with the courage, good temper, resource, patience, and, if I may say so, optimism with which you have played the game on both sides of the Atlantic... You are going to exchange the misery of obstruction for the buoyancy of construction.*

Southborough to Taylor, June 17, 1936

56

Rendering of the bridge, 1936.

In 1937 Taylor was interviewed on BBC Radio, and told the broadcast audience about his humble beginnings in Vancouver. In describing the Marine Building, he claimed 'I own the flat in the tower of that building, actually overlooking my old eight-shillings-a-month shack, still standing, in which I lived as a boy. I can therefore truly claim to have risen four hundred feet in the world.' The shack is still to be seen on the bluff just to the right of the centre foreground of this 1935 photograph of the Marine Building.

*The whole dwelling is a successful combination of pure fantasy and twentieth century comfort. Mr. Taylor has created a small world of his own in the sky. On a wide paved terrace, he can enjoy sun, air, exercise and the changing panorama of the countryside. It is unbelievable that he should ever be tempted to descend to earth again.*

The top floor of the Marine Building, the nineteenth, was reserved by Taylor for the offices of British Pacific Properties. This floor was reached by a private four person elevator. The crowning feature of the building was a lookout tower, which had only been open for a few months as the public was not willing, or not able, to pay to see the view. The space stood empty until Taylor decided to build a palatial penthouse for his own use. He had always wanted to live in a house 'above the shop' so as to be closer to his work. This 'skyscraper home' was used by Taylor for hosting business luncheons and out-of-town guests, and was a far cry from the CPR shack he had shared at virtually the same location in 1903.

This stunningly elegant penthouse was one of the only ones ever built in Vancouver, and resembled a movie set more than a home. Architectural advice on the design had been solicited from Taylor's friend C. Howard Crane, from a Mr. Dorey of Los Angeles, and locally from Palmer & Bow. Lavishly appointed in jazzy Art Deco style, the living room reached the full seventeen foot height of the tower, with a mezzanine inserted for two upstairs bedrooms. The floor of this living room was raised several steps to increase access to the panoramic view. The black marble fireplace, mahogany fittings, wood panelled walls and teak floors were the height of contemporary style. The enormous chandelier in the living room was a copy of one in Rockefeller Center, each lamp fitted with a reflector cup to provide indirect illumination.

But the Taylor family never moved in. Due to the lack of convenience and community, Mona rented a home in Caulfeild in West Vancouver until the family's new residence, *Kew House*, was finished. Taylor sometimes used the penthouse to avoid the long commute home. He lived here again only briefly, towards the end of the war. It was later converted to office space, and remains virtually intact. The living room is currently used as a corporate boardroom.

## THE PENTHOUSE

The Marine Building Penthouse, March 12, 1936.

October 17, 1937

# KEW HOUSE

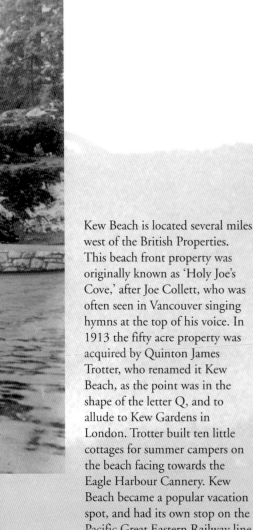

Kew Beach is located several miles west of the British Properties. This beach front property was originally known as 'Holy Joe's Cove,' after Joe Collett, who was often seen in Vancouver singing hymns at the top of his voice. In 1913 the fifty acre property was acquired by Quinton James Trotter, who renamed it Kew Beach, as the point was in the shape of the letter Q, and to allude to Kew Gardens in London. Trotter built ten little cottages for summer campers on the beach facing towards the Eagle Harbour Cannery. Kew Beach became a popular vacation spot, and had its own stop on the Pacific Great Eastern Railway line. Taylor 'took a fancy' to the property, and in September, 1936, bought the twenty-four acres west of the PGE line. He had five different architects prepare plans for a sumptuous home before settling on those of Palmer & Bow.

Bernard Cuddon Palmer and William Bow were well-known designers of many lavish homes, and had already undertaken a number of commissions for Taylor, included the first building in the British Properties, the Company Cottage. Bernard Palmer died unexpectedly in 1936, at the age of 60, but Bow retained the name of the partnership and continued his ongoing commissions for Taylor, including the design of *Kew House*.

Taylor wanted the house to look as 'Mediterranean' as possible, and insisted on a blush of pink in the wall colour. He shopped in Italy for items for the house, which he shipped back as construction proceeded. After the house was complete, it was the scene of many great events and much entertaining, including nobility such as Lord and Lady Tweedsmuir. *Kew House* was not Taylor's only indulgence at this time. He had also purchased Samuel Island, which faces the east end of Saturna, as a summer residence, and ordered himself a new luxury yacht.

In 1943 *Kew House* and Samuel Island were sold to Garfield Weston, who planned to take possession after the end of the war. Weston, a Toronto born British MP and a personal friend of Taylor's, was known as the 'Biscuit King.' He was one of the wealthiest men in the British Empire, and had decided to establish his home in Vancouver.

William Bow, Architect, 1882-1956.

# PART TWO

*'Sure she's a good bridge; a mighty good bridge,' he sang out over the roar of riveting machines, as he reached for a section of steel truss work dangling at the end of a derrick's hoisting chain... 'And a pretty bridge. Light and graceful, like a spider's web in the sun.'*

**Joe Lepage, bridge workman**

THIS WEB OF STEEL

THE CONSTRUCTION OF A GREAT BRIDGE is a very complicated feat of engineering. Its structure must be pared to a minimum but still resist tremendous and constantly moving loads. Unlike a building, which is built from the bottom up and where gravity is the main concern, every component of a bridge must also support itself until the entire structure is assembled. The process of construction becomes a unique puzzle, juggling complex requirements and balancing enormous components until the structure is complete and hangs together as a unit. Building a bridge is one of the most daring acts of construction, and has always inspired the public imagination.

Given the romance of such an enterprise, the creation of a great suspension bridge erected in the most highly visible spot in a metropolitan area was sure to become a great public event. Daily, the progress of the Lions Gate Bridge was monitored and commented on. This was the best show in town, and free for the viewing.

*Most amazing of all, this web of steel spanning the narrow fairway, stately as a cathedral, enduring as the hills above it, yet delicate and airy as a song.*

Canada's leading bridge design firm, Montreal-based Monsarrat & Pratley, were retained by The First Narrows Bridge Company for the design and supervision of the construction of the bridge. Major W.G. Swan, consulting engineer, was their Vancouver representative, and was responsible for preliminary surveys and planning. Robinson & Steinman of New York City were retained in an advisory capacity with regard to certain features, such as the bridge lighting. Architect John W. Wood was retained to provide designs for the aesthetic features of the bridge. The design team proved themselves worthy of the task, for the bridge was groundbreaking in many aspects. We can only wonder at the complexity of the calculations, which at the time had to be undertaken with nothing more than a slide rule.

**Timber!**
Construction officially began on **March 31, 1937** when a gang of men started clearing the 66 foot right-of-way through Stanley Park. A total of ten acres of the park was cleared, with care taken to preserve the larger and finer trees. The North Shore approaches were also cleared, and the brush burned before the dry weather set in.

## CLEARING THE ROADWAY

**April 21, 1937**

**August 3, 1937**

A construction plant was started at the south bridgehead on **April 9, 1937**. The main part of the plant was built on top of the cliff at Prospect Point, and the lower part of the plant was built on the beach below. Materials were brought to the site by barge.

## SOUTH PLANT

On **April 15, 1937**, work commenced on driving piles for the two rock cribs that were used in preparing foundations for the derricks. A long timber float between the cribs acted as a breakwater to form a quiet area for the underwater work.

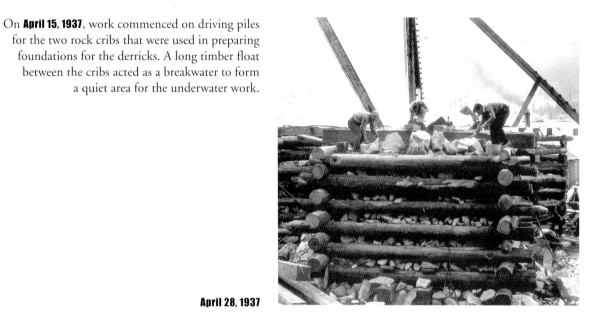

**April 28, 1937**

Blasting started on **June 24, 1937** to level off the seabed. A slight jar and a few bubbles was all that marked the explosion of six charges of dynamite on the floor of the Narrows. The caissons, each forty-eight feet in diameter by forty-one feet high, were constructed of steel, concrete and timber, assembled on the bank, and floated off at high tide to be completed. Each caisson weighed 172 tons when launched and concrete was added to bring their weight up to 2,180 tons before they were grounded in their final position.

**October 6, 1937**

**September 1, 1937**

70

**October 31, 1937**

SOUTH PIER FOUNDATIONS

### *Here is a Western 'HE-MAN'S' idea of bricklaying!*

Monsarrat & Pratley specified granite facings for the portions of the piers above the water. This was the usual treatment where ice conditions prevailed. The Bridge Company proposed in 1937 that the granite facings be left off, and the piers left as bare concrete, so that the money saved could be spent on improvements to Stanley Park. Taylor reported to City Council that this would allow for more impressive approaches, including 'huge stone lions or Indians, with a plaza and seating accommodation for those who come to the bridgehead for a view of the Lions Gate.' After weeks of debate, and a storm of protest from interested parties including suppliers and masons, the company went ahead with the planned stone facings. Granite blocks from Nelson Island, B.C. were used to face the piers. A total of 816 pieces were used and the average weight of each piece was four tons.

72

## SOUTH PIER FACINGS

The tower shoes were built of steel slabs welded together. Each shoe weighed 18 tons and rested on a double layer of heavily painted canvas. They were each anchored to the pier by twenty-eight bolts. Workers and engineers placed all their small change, amounting to thirty-five cents, below the foot of the first steel.

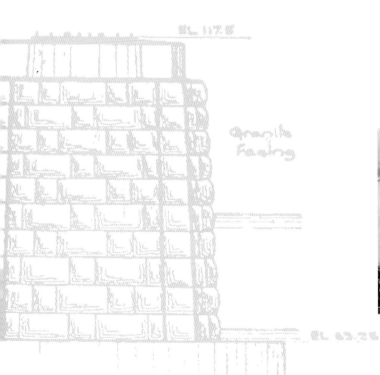

**TOWER SHOES**

Construction was simultaneously underway on the north viaduct and the north pier foundations. The north plant was started with a material and construction dock built on the beach. The caisson for the north pier was a huge bottomless concrete box that weighed 8,700 tons. It was sunk starting on **August 13, 1937**, by dredging material from the inside. As the interior was dredged out, the caisson was held in place by exterior surface friction, calculated to be as high as 450 pounds per square inch. Blasting charges had to be set off to destroy the surface friction and allow the caisson to settle into place. It reached its designed elevation, seventy-two feet below its starting point, in exactly three months' time.

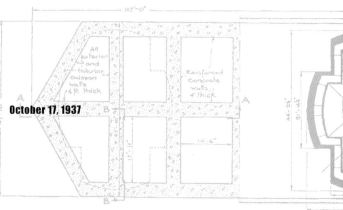

**October 17, 1937**

**NORTH PIER FOUNDATION**

The North Shore approach required a concrete abutment that formed the end of the gravel fill and marked the starting point of the north viaduct steelwork. It was later covered by fill.

76

Concrete pedestal foundations were poured for the steel supports of the viaduct, seen here looking north from the PGE tracks towards the concrete abutment.

October 17, 1937.

# NORTH VIADUCT

**November 4, 1937**

On the North Shore approach a 2,196 foot long viaduct had to be built to raise the roadbed to the required height. A movable hoisting tower, 120 feet high with a 75 foot boom, was constructed on a rail system to lift material on the north side. The first steel was erected on the north viaduct on **November 25, 1937.**

In order to bring the roadway to the desired height as quickly as possible, the maximum permissible gradient, almost five percent, was employed. The spans increased in spacing as the viaduct rose, in order to provide satisfactory proportions to the appearance of the structure.

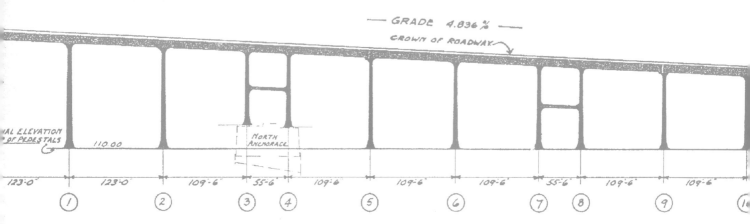

GRADE 4.836 %

CROWN OF ROADWAY

AL ELEVATION OF PEDESTALS

110.00

NORTH ANCHORAGE

123'-0"  123'-0"  109'-6"  55'-6"  109'-6"  109'-6"  109'-6"  55'-6"  109'-6"  109'-6"

① ② ③ ④ ⑤ ⑥ ⑦ ⑧ ⑨ ①

## NORTH VIADUCT

Right: **April 20, 1938**

**December 8, 1937**

The north anchor block was thirty feet by seventy-four feet in plan, and forty-four feet deep. It weighed 20,000 tons, and was designed to withstand a maximum cable pull of 6,300 tons. The block was positioned to act as the footing for two legs of the viaduct, so that the weight of the structure would help resist the pull of the suspension cables.

NORTH ANCHORAGE

The tower sections, weighing up to 22 tons each, were fabricated at the Dominion Bridge Company's Burnaby plant. They were shipped by rail and scow to the site, then hoisted into place using a 25 ton capacity Creeper Traveller. The Creeper was a stiff leg derrick with a thirty foot mast and a fifty foot boom, which could 'jump' higher as the tower rose. Erection of the south tower started first. Assembly of the Creeper began on **January 18, 1938**.

82

## CREEPER TRAVELLER

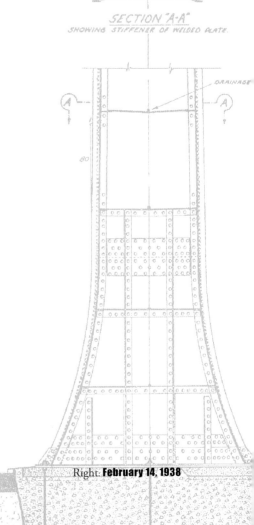

*SECTION "A-A"*
*SHOWING STIFFENER OF WELDED PLATE*

Right: **February 14, 1938**

On **March 10, 1938** the south tower was completed. The Creeper Traveller was dismantled, and transferred to the north side.

**SOUTH TOWER**

**March 30, 1938**

**March 31, 1938**

# NORTH TOWER

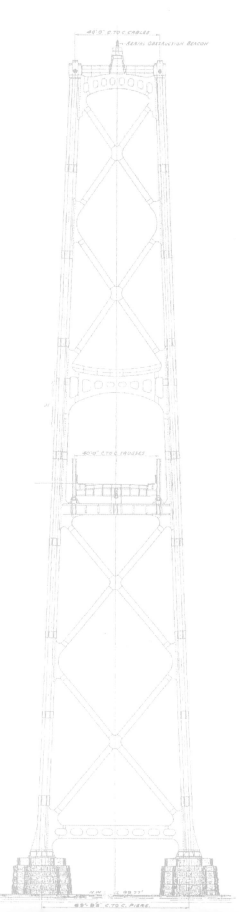

On **March 23, 1938**, assembly started on the Creeper on the north side. Work on the north tower was finished on **April 29, 1938**. Each completed tower was 364 feet in height from the top of the masonry piers.

Painting quickly followed
the erection of the steel.
This painter worked on the
North Shore viaduct using
a spray-gun.

The Narrows were closed to shipping for the first time ever, to allow the catwalk cables to be hoisted. While engineers superintended from a launch, a barge travelled north, paying out the cables from a huge reel at its stern. Despite the hazards of tide and currents, the Narrows were open to traffic again in little more than an hour. Each cable weighed eight tons, with four cables to each catwalk. The cables were hoisted to the top of each of the towers, and anchored three feet below where the main cables were to be located.

Right: **6:00 a.m., May 2, 1938**

**5:23 a.m., May 2, 1938**

# HOISTING THE CATWALK CABLES

*Vancouver Daily Province*, **May 3, 1938**

The catwalks were footbridges hung three feet below where the main cables would be placed. Although not part of the structure of the bridge, they were crucial to its construction, acting as the equivalent of scaffolding. Starting at the north tower, the individual sections of the catwalks were slid into place on the cables, and the first man walked across just 8 ½ days later.

94

## BUILDING THE CATWALKS

**May 31, 1938**

95

**May 18, 1938**

The most significant innovation for this bridge was the use of prefabricated strands for the suspension cables. Prior to this, cables had been wound on site. Each cable strand for this project was fabricated from 47 prestressed wires supplied by an American firm, John A. Roebling's Sons Co. The wires were twisted into 3,400 foot long strands by the Anglo-Canadian Wire Rope Co. of Lachine, Quebec. They were prestretched at the factory, and hollow steel end sockets were attached by pouring molten zinc into the cavity. The cable strands were then wound onto wooden spools four feet in diameter and shipped by rail to Vancouver. The cable spools were placed at the north side, and each strand was hauled over the catwalks with a ⅝ inch line by means of a hoisting engine at the south anchor pier. They were attached to 'button anchors' by adjustable bolts, then hoisted into place on the tower saddles. Final tightening was accomplished by two men with wrenches, who 'tuned' each strand like a piano wire, tapping it until it sounded at the right frequency. All 122 cable strands were in place in sixteen working days. The long hours of daylight permitted three working shifts, the third shift of each day being devoted to adjusting the strands for length.

**HAULING THE CABLE STRANDS**

The company that manufactured the wires for the cable strands and the suspender ropes had been founded by the famous Roebling family of bridge builders. John A. Roebling was the designer of the Brooklyn Bridge, the most heroic structure built during the 19th century, and the first suspension bridge to be built of steel rather than iron. The bridge was years in construction. Roebling was killed in an accident at the site in 1869, and his son Washington A. Roebling took over the project. The younger Roebling was invalided three years later from an attack of the bends while working in a caisson under the East River, but he managed to oversee construction from his home in Brooklyn Heights, by means of a telescope, and by relaying messages to the assistant engineer through his wife Emily. The Brooklyn Bridge was finally completed in 1883, after fourteen years of construction. The company the Roeblings founded remained prominent for many decades as a leading bridge design and construction firm.

Reels 57 to 73 incl.  } Alike
Reels 92 to 122 incl. }
For Right Hand Lay

Right Hand

57  58

51  52  5

Right Hand          44  45  46

36  37  38  3

Right Hand      27  28  29  30

19  20  21  2

Right Hand          12  13  14

Suspender
Guide Strand
Reels 58 78 or 79            6  7  8

Right Hand          1  2

The natural grouping of parallel round strands is hexagonal, and this shape can only be achieved by using one of the series 1, 7, 19, 37, 61, 91, 127, etc. The number of cable strands in the final cable must be a balance between undue stiffness and too cumbersome an anchorage. For this bridge, a cable bundle of 61 individual strands, each 1.44 inches in diameter, was chosen.

The southern anchor pier was a wedge-shaped block, weighing about 15,000 tons and sunk forty feet deep in hard clay. Each cable strand was attached to a steel 'button anchor.' Four splay collars, each weighing 900 pounds, were used to guide the strands into their radial position, while avoiding any abrupt changes in alignment. The only fatal accident during the bridge construction was due to a cave-in on the south anchor pit when a mucker, Lester Thorstad, was crushed by falling debris.

100

Casting-75D.

SOUTH ANCHORAGE

The strands were made in Lachine, Que., and no cutting was done at the bridge site— a process that made exactitude in preliminary preparation a first essential. But regardless of that, the laying of those strands to form the main cables was a complex and difficult undertaking. In the heat of the day the strands near the top of the mass would writhe like huge reptiles. They would expand and sag, buckle and twist, and drop between the lower, cooler ones. So the work had to be done when the temperature was uniform, usually at night under the glare of floodlights. As the strands were finally set in place, they were clamped securely together to form two master cables to bear the weight of the bridge. "There were times when the bridge really seemed alive," said one of the engineers. "We couldn't do a thing with those cables during the day if the sun was shining. The only thing we could do was to stage our taming act at night".

102

## CLAMPING THE CABLE STRANDS

*Across the Lions' Gate, the ruggedly beautiful channel which marks the sea approach to British Columbia's metropolis, these men have been wrestling with the gigantic steel web that constitutes the British Empire's longest suspension bridge.*

The cable strands were clamped with 166 large steel cable bands, cast by Vancouver Engineering Works Ltd. Each cable band consisted of a symmetrical pair of castings, which were bolted into place. The angle of the saddle-groove for each band varied in accordance with its location on the cable, and had to be calculated to within three degrees so that the suspender ropes would hang properly.

103

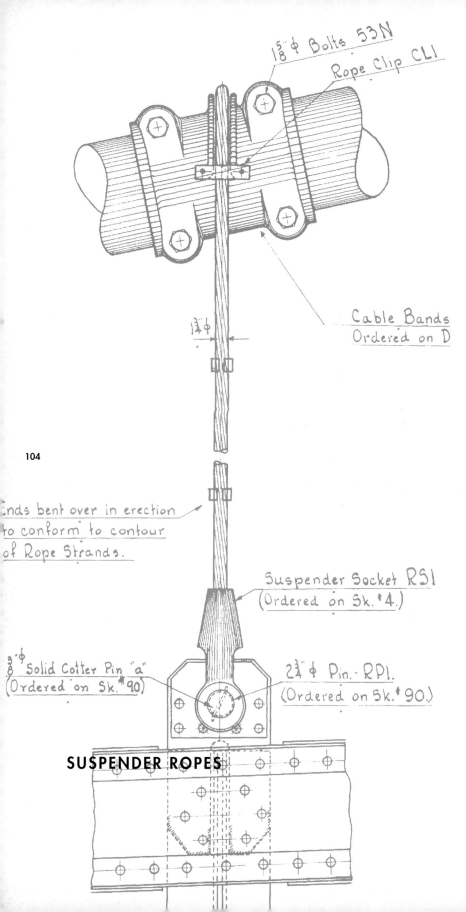

1⅝" φ Bolts 53N

Rope Clip CL1

Cable Bands
Ordered on D

1¾φ

104

Ends bent over in erection
to conform to contour
of Rope Strands.

Suspender Socket RS1
(Ordered on Sk. #4.)

⅜"φ Solid Cotter Pin "a"
(Ordered on Sk. #90)

2¼"φ Pin. RP1.
(Ordered on Sk. #90.)

**SUSPENDER ROPES**

The cable bands acted as saddles
for the steel suspender ropes. Each
suspender was manufactured from 163
separate wires, with a final diameter of
1 ¾ inches. They were allowed to hang
free until the stiffening trusses were
placed.

**June 9, 1938**

The first section of the steel roadbed, known as a 'Warren' truss, was raised from a scow to the centre of the span by a steam hoist on shore. Due to the tide, the scow made two attempts before it was correctly positioned for the load to be hoisted. In twelve days 174 sections, weighing 1,572 tons, were in place.

107

STIFFENING TRUSSES

**June 9, 1938**

The 'bump' in the middle of the bridge, sometimes explained as a mistake made during construction, was a result of the bridge's economical design. The road profile allowed the required clearance of 200 feet at the centre of the bridge, but descended on each side in almost straight lines instead of the usual circular curve.

**June 24, 1938**

By **June 29, 1938** it was possible to commence the laying of the floor system, starting with the floor beams, then the stringers. Welded sections of steel Tee grid were secured on top to form the roadbed.

111

Evelyn Caldwell, a well-known local journalist, started her forty-four year long career as a journalist at the Vancouver *Star* in 1929. She later worked for eleven years at the *News-Herald*, where she wrote a column called *Sauce for the Goose*, and covered provincial politics. She joined the *Sun* September 1, 1945, writing under the name Penny Wise. Caldwell travelled extensively, including to Monaco in 1956, to cover the wedding of Prince Rainier II and Grace Kelly, and to Memphis that same year to interview a young Elvis Presley. She died in 1998 at the age of 89. In addition to her many other achievements, she was the first woman to cross the Lions Gate Bridge. This article appeared in the *Vancouver News-Herald* on August 30, 1938.

## THRILLS AND PERILS TO BE FIRST WOMAN ACROSS THE BRIDGE

By Evelyn A. Caldwell

'Surely you're not going to walk over the cat-walk in those high-heels.'

And the good-looking youngish man who is in charge of engineering on the Lions' Gate Bridge looked disapprovingly at my slim-heeled pumps when I confronted him in a little rough-wood office on the south end of the bridge.

'The c-c-c-cat w-w-w-w-walk?' I stammered, batting an eye no end. 'Am I going to walk over the cat-walk?'

'Why, I thought that was what you wanted to do,' H. Minshall said, 'but you can suit yourself, of course—if you don't think you'd care to go up there its O.K. with me...'

'Oh, I'd like to go over it alright,' I hastened to say in case he might change his mind and not want a woman traipsing over his bridge.

'I just didn't think you'd let me go over the cat-walk,' I explained. 'But I did want to be the first woman to walk over the bridge—sure I'll go over the top.'

After all, I reminded myself, the bridge-walking idea was mine and I might just as well be stuck properly with it—only—I didn't dare look up the 400 feet to the tower.

\* \* \*

Thus I let myself in for an exciting morning adventure, for walk over the cat-walk I did—the whole swaying way across the swirling waters of The Narrows, and back I came across the slightly sloping, partly paved road-bed of the new structure.

'Fools,' they say, 'walk in where angels fear to tread,' and, while I didn't feel particularly sensible as I started up the narrow, boarded 45-degree path to the first cable tower one-thirteenth of a mile above, before I was at the top I felt I would have been foolish to have welshed at the chance of crossing the bridge that way.

Preceded by a newspaper photographer who was in his element at the opportunity afforded for wonderful pictures, and followed by the engineer to whom the climb was as uneventful as a walk down Granville Street, and an enthusiastic amateur candid-cameraman, I started the 400-foot climb, passing the space where they're building the foundation for the two huge lions that will guard the south-end entrance to the bridge.

Before we had gone thirty steps along the hen-coop studded walk, we were above the tops of the highest trees in Stanley Park, and row-boats on The Narrows were tiny things.

With both hands I clung to the cable hand-rail, listening the while to our well-versed guide tell us about the huge 61-strand cable that went up the centre of the cat-walk, about how the first one was brought across the

Narrows and tapped and laid, then another and another, until the whole 61 were set in a great sexagonal [sic] suspension rope.

Then we were half-way to the top of the first tower.

The workmen below were hoo-hooing us and shaking their knees in sympathy.

They should shake their knees—mine needed no encouragement; and I couldn't wave to them—too busy hanging on with both hands for dear life.

The amateur cameraman was too, so I didn't feel too badly, and the other two refrained from rubbing in the fact that they weren't hanging on at all, at all—their hands were clean; mine quarter-inch thick with grease from the cable.

Two-thirds of the way up and I hadn't looked down for many a step past despite repeated suggestions to 'Look at the skyline of the city from here;' 'See the new road through the Park;' 'See Vancouver Island;' 'Look at British Properties;' 'Watch the West Vancouver Ferry go under.'

I could only see the swaying cat-walk and the greasy hand-rail, and at the moment they were more to me than all the skylines, all the new roads, all the islands and all the ferries in the world—well in Vancouver, anyway. If I stopped, or looked, or even listened too hard, I knew I'd sit down right there and refuse to move, and they'd have a wretched reporter guarding their bridge, along with the two lions.

* * *

And so, before I knew it, I was at the top, right alongside the tall pillar that will house the strong beacon light when the bridge is finished. The top of the tower had a floor, of sorts, across it, and I could stand there and look at the floor without seeing any water or any land, and after doing that for a while, I managed a peek over, found I liked it, and from then on the thing was a cinch and I became bridge-climber par excellence.

I leaned over rails and watched freight boats pass underneath, en route to goodness knows what far-distant ports; watched fishermen standing at the mouth of the Capilano waiting for bites; saw the view, unsurpassable in its magnificence; saw the three portions of cement on the road-bed of the bridge far below; saw everything that could be seen from that lofty 400-foot perch.

Then crossed over and started down the not-so-steep slope on the other side, heading towards the centre of the bridge to the point where the signals will be placed—the signals that have directed in and out-going traffic from Prospect Point for many years. Then up again to the top of the north-side tower, and once more down, this time onto the road-bed of the bridge and back the 5000 feet of its slightly sloping length to the starting point—the first woman to make such a trip.

Mr. Minshall told me all I wanted to know about the bridge—except when it would be finished. He couldn't say exactly, but did say the exceptional weather of the past summer had been most helpful in promoting work on the structure and that not more than one week's work had been lost since the beginning of the engineering work.

He told me that when the south tower was finished the two sides were but three-eighths of an inch out of plumb—a miracle in engineering feats, and he pointed out the roadbed was a two car one, with passage room; that there would be pedestrian sidewalks on both sides with seated view-balconies at four vantage points for sight-seers.

He showed me how the workers were making ladders of the suspended cables and said nearly 9000 rungs would be installed before the bridge was completed; and when three bottle-green paint-covered men appeared in sight, he said that would be the colour of the bridge which would be fenced in on both sides by galvanized fencing and lighted by the new fog-proof lamps.

* * *

Heretofore the bridge, to me, had been nothing but a means of getting from Stanley Park to West Vancouver. Now it was a matter of men who dealt in the 2000th part of an inch, and in many-tonned beams of iron.

It was a matter of daring men who took their lives in their hands every day and thought nothing about it; of men who walked across slanted beams 300 feet above the sea just to get a light for a cigarette; of men who threw red-hot rivets around like adept jugglers; of men who took every emergency in their stride; of men whose business was—building bridges.

No bridge of sighs, that Lions' Gate, but a bridge of heights and sights—unforgettable heights, unforgettable sights.

Don Jamieson sitting on the cables.

Starting on **August 16, 1938** the Tee grid system was filled with three inches of concrete to form the road surface. This was a relatively simple job, for the welded sections acted as the forms for the slab. The pouring was done in sections, working simultaneously from either end of the span, to avoid unequal loading that would overstress the cables. This allowed the cables to be gradually brought up to their full design load, stretching them into their appropriate position. Concrete pouring was completed on **September 23, 1938**.

A total of 8,800 ladder rungs were hammered into place at 15 inch intervals between the suspender ropes, starting on **August 18, 1938**. These rungs provided access to the cables for maintenance and inspection.

**September 30, 1938**

## ROADBED

**September 23, 1938**

Once the cables were fully loaded, they were encased with cedar filler strips to form a cylindrical shape. They were then wrapped with soft galvanized No. 9 wire by an air-driven rotary machine. The cables and suspender ropes were painted *International Aviation Red* so that they would be highly visible to aircraft. The rest of the steelwork was painted a rich olive green, except for the underside of the of the suspended spans, which were painted in a dark brown colour.

Left: Painters and electricians put the finishing touches on the bridge. The cable-wrapping machine is at work on the left catwalk. **October 19, 1938**

# FINISHING TOUCHES

**September 21, 1938**

Montreal based architect John Wilson Wood was responsible for the design of the anchor piers, pylons and statue bases of the bridge. Born in Kilmarnock, Scotland on January 13, 1885, he received his architectural training before he emigrated to Canada in 1908. From 1911 to 1933 he was a principal in the office of Hugh G. Jones, one of the associated architects for Toronto's Union Station. The next five years he served as principal assistant to Roper & Morin in Ottawa, undertaking mostly domestic work. He was hired in 1938 by the office of the Chief Architect of the Canadian National Railway, and worked there until his retirement on large projects such as the Central Station and the Queen Elizabeth Hotel in Montreal; he died in 1965. Wood likely became involved in the Lions Gate Bridge project through Monsarrat & Pratley. As the anchor piers were part of the structure of the bridge, he would have worked closely with the engineers on their design. The Administration Building and the toll gates at the north end of the bridge (right) were designed by local architects Palmer & Bow under a separate contract.

**January 25, 1939**

# THE PYLONS

Open to cars: **November 14, 1938**

The bridge was finished months ahead of its original schedule, due to excellent weather conditions and the meticulous planning and scheduling of the engineers. It was opened to pedestrian traffic on **Saturday, November 12, 1938**. Two days later the bridge was opened to cars. At the car opening Philip Curry (left) sold Ticket #1 to Reeve Joseph B. Leyland of West Vancouver (centre), and Ticket #2 to Mayor George C. Miller of Vancouver (right).

**January 31, 1939**

**OPEN FOR TRAFFIC**

# PART THREE

*It is much more than a bridge between Vancouver and the
North Shore. It is the bridge to better times.*

*Vancouver Daily Province,* April 30, 1936

SYMBOL OF EMPIRE

*Lions' Gate Bridge is a symbol and a memorial: Symbol of Empire, memorial to the men of faith and foresight who made its construction possible. These men include, besides prophets and leaders of opinion in Vancouver who struggled long years to attain their ideal of a bridge to connect the City of Vancouver on the south side of this harbour with its North Shore suburbs, and the group of British capitalists whose financial backing made the ideal at last attainable. That ideal took form in the longest suspension bridge in the British Empire, the longest suspension bridge of stranded type in the world.*

THE CONSTRUCTION OF THE BRIDGE was relatively trouble free, but this was not reflected in the board room at British Pacific Properties. While Taylor's achievements promised the company great wealth, his personal success was viewed with some distrust. His side deals and investments, especially in other West Vancouver real estate ventures, provided potential competition. Another concern was the lacklustre performance of sales at the British Properties. Early in the game, Taylor had planned to build his family home in the Properties, but the company had inexplicably refused to approve it. This petty move persuaded him to buy the Kew Beach property, which was perceived as a lack of confidence in his own development.

*The Guinnesses had always shown more tenacity in their grip on the boardroom seats than was the case with other founding families of comparably great public companies.*

127

The Guinnesses were undoubtedly concerned about their extensive investments in Vancouver. Despite growing excitement about the bridge, few were willing to actually buy property in the new subdivision, and the Properties languished. Taylor's mammoth labours on the company's behalf were obvious, but his loyalty was to his projects rather than his British investors. Rumours were relayed to England that Taylor was using British Pacific Properties funds for his own purposes, and Taylor met with the Guinnesses in London to answer these charges. Even though the rumours were petty and malicious, Taylor quarrelled with C.H. Bland, the head of the London office, and the atmosphere became increasingly divisive and hostile. Southborough remained loyal to Taylor, but was a long distance participant, and rarely left London. Early in 1938 the Guinnesses sent a personal representative, L. Peter Candler, to initiate 'definite plans for marketing.' Candler had been living in Montreal for four years, managing other large investments of the Guinness family. He had been assisted in his work by A.M.J. English, Vancouver Manager of the Royal Trust Company of Montreal, and for several years a Director of British Pacific Properties.

Candler, in an attempt to start selling the lots, met with the executive of the Vancouver Real Estate Exchange. English was a former President of the Exchange, and was able to assist both sides in reaching an agreement, in which the Properties would be marketed locally through Exchange members. Sales would now be made by private real estate agents rather than through the development company. Taylor and Anderson were completely opposed to this shift in focus, and resigned from the board on March 9, 1938, the day the new marketing plan was announced. One week later, the Manager of the Properties, Robert W. Keyserlingk, declared at a luncheon meeting at the Real Estate Exchange 'We used the depression for preparation. We will now use the time of recovery for marketing.'

Two months later Southborough also resigned from the Board of British Pacific Properties. Taylor and Anderson remained involved with both the Bridge Company and the management of the Marine Building, but further complications soon developed. In July 1938, Major Philip Arthur Curry, O.B.E., long associated with the Canadian branch of the White Star Line, was brought from Montreal to act as General Manager of the Properties, and was also installed as General Managing Director of the Bridge Company. Construction of the bridge was being rushed through to completion; no official date of opening was announced, as the company did not wish to miss any stated deadline, even though it was actually ahead of schedule. Taylor refused to walk away from the bridge project, but Curry, jealous of Taylor's business successes, became a constant irritant. The bridge was opened to traffic in November of 1938, but Taylor stayed on until May of the following year to ensure that final completion was to his satisfaction.

*The announcement which recently appeared in the local press informing the public as to a proposed change in the management of the British Pacific Properties came as a complete surprise,—in fact, one may say that to the Municipal Council of West Vancouver it was somewhat of a shock and was received with the deepest regret.*
Reeve Leyland to Lord Southborough,
March 16, 1938

One finishing touch yet to be taken care of was the installation of the grand Lions sculptures at the south entry to the bridge. These monumental figures were the last and greatest public work of Vancouver's foremost sculptor, Charles Marega. The figures were first sculpted in clay, then cast in plaster, from which the final moulds were made. The choice of material dictated the bold style of the Lions, as concrete cannot be cast with delicate details or undercuts. Beautifully and intensely modelled in an abstracted Art Deco style, they were an appropriate and fitting symbol of power to both guard and anchor the south end of the bridge. Superbly integrated with the structure of the entry pylons and the bridge itself, their supreme confidence conveyed a message of stability and better times ahead. The artistic success of these sculptures is undeniable, and they were a remarkable culmination to Marega's career.

The Lions were lifted onto their pylons by crane in January of 1939. Cast in two pieces by Stuart Cameron & Company, each body weighed six and one-half tons, and each head, two tons. Marega was not in attendance when the bodies were hoisted, as he was reportedly too nervous to watch, in case something happened. Two miniature versions of the Lions were cast in concrete and given to Taylor, who placed them at his summer home on Samuel Island.

The official opening of the bridge finally took place on May 26, 1939. In a 'happy little ceremony' the bridge was formally handed over to Taylor. A procession of automobiles carried seventy dignitaries from the Stanley Park Pavilion, across the new bridge, and up the winding roads of the British Properties to the Capilano Golf Clubhouse. Taylor was presented with a certificate, signed by Dr. Pratley, that the bridge had been completed to the satisfaction of the consulting engineers. In his acceptance speech Taylor thanked those responsible.

*Today is free of all regrets but one. I am sorry that many of our friends who have helped to make the bridge possible are unable to be here. In particular, I regret the absence of Lord Southborough. To him I owe more than to any other living person.*

*I should especially like you all to know that, in a lifetime of contracting experience, I have never known a major enterprise like the Lions' Gate Bridge that was so free from natural and human troubles during construction. I can truthfully say that, so far as the contractors are concerned throughout the entire vast process, we have not had occasion for a single unkind word, written or spoken.*

*A lusty child has been born, richly endowed in capacity to render service for long years ahead. Unlike a human child, it cannot be spoilt by neglect or even by a complete disregard of its spiritual significance. It will go on contributing to the happiness of millions long after its creators are buried and forgotten. With this confidence in its future and without regrets, I am moving on at once to other constructive works within this great Province we are proud to call home.*

Taylor and Anderson then immediately resigned from the bridge company. Few had seen the extent of Taylor's struggle, or the pain it had caused him. Now that his greatest achievement was complete, he left to embark on other grand ventures. The bridge, and its guardian Lions which concealed his enigmatic story, would stand as his symbol of a new kind of Empire.

*Thank God I have work now. I am modelling a lion for Vancouver's suspension bridge. I had much trouble to get the work. The engineer is from Montreal and wanted the lion to be modelled in Montreal. But the president of the bridge committee, who is a long-standing friend of mine, and his wife, was a good friend of mama's, finally assigned the work to me. I would have preferred the lions to be in bronze or stone—but it had to be cheap, so they will be done in concrete, which annoys me, as I could otherwise have made both lions from one model. However I have to content myself to get work at all.*

Letter from Charles Marega to his in-laws in August 1938

Charles Marega, the first and best known of Vancouver's professional sculptors, has left his mark on this city in stone, bronze and concrete. It was said at his funeral that 'there is no need to build him a monument—because of his sculpture he will never be forgotten.'

Originally named Carlos, he was born on September 24, 1871 in Lucinico, in the commune of Gorizia near Trieste, then part of the Austro-Hungarian Empire. Marega and his wife Berta were on their way to California in October 1909 when they passed through Vancouver. Staying at the Hotel Vancouver, when they woke up the next morning, the view north towards the mountains on a fine sunny fall day so reminded Berta of her native Switzerland that they decided to stay. Their timing was excellent. These were Vancouver's boom years, and as the most proficient local architectural sculptor and decorator, Marega soon attracted notice, and numerous commissions. During the First World War the work dried up, but afterward Marega was again busy. In 1925 the Vancouver School of Decorative and Applied Arts opened, and Marega was hired to teach sculpture, a part-time position he held until his death.

The onset of the Great Depression brought tough times for Marega. He did secure some high profile work, such as many of the motifs for the Marine Building, the statuary for the new Vancouver Art Gallery on Georgia Street in 1931 and the sculptural decoration on the Burrard Bridge, opened in 1932, but these commissions did not appear with the same frequency as before. His beloved wife Berta, whom he referred to as mama, died in 1934, a blow from which he never fully recovered.

Ironically, this low point in his life was a time of artistic triumph. His good friend Fred Townley, the architect of Vancouver City Hall, ensured that he received the commission for a statue of Captain George Vancouver, which was unveiled by the Lord Mayor of London on August 20, 1936. Despite his many commissions, Marega died almost penniless. On March 27, 1939, just months after the Lions were finished, he collapsed and died of a heart attack at the Vancouver School of Art.

# CHARLES MAREGA

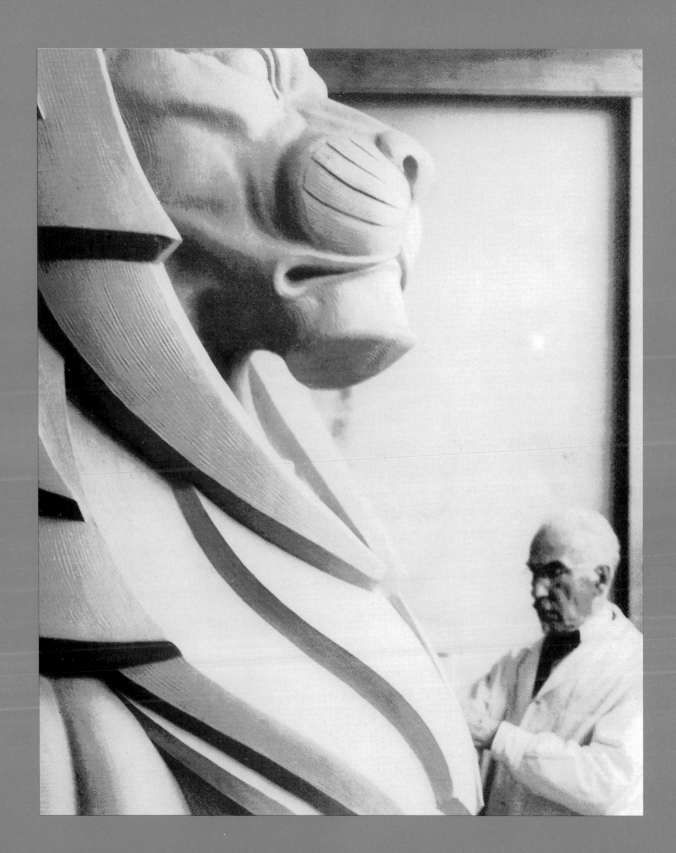

The King and Queen 'honoured' the bridge on May 29, 1939.

Three days after the bridge was officially handed over to Taylor, King George VI and Queen Elizabeth arrived in Vancouver as part of their tour of the colonies. This was the first time that reigning British monarchs had visited Canada; the preparations were extensive, and the public appetite to participate was unlimited. As part of the itinerary, the Royals were to spend one day in Vancouver. Arriving by CPR train from the East, they toured the west side in the morning, with a stop at City Hall. A lunch for civic dignitaries was held at the Hotel Vancouver at 1 p.m., following which they headed through East Vancouver and over the Second Narrows Bridge to the North Shore. There were few scheduled stops, as they had to cover fifty-seven miles at a speed not to exceed 20 miles per hour. Virtually all requests for extra stops had been refused.

One afternoon rest stop was added at the last minute, a tea break at the British Properties Company Cottage below Eyremount Drive. To avoid the appearance of the Royals accepting private hospitality, the cottage was placed in the hands of West Vancouver municipality for the day. This allowed the King and Queen a chance to get out of the car, accept refreshments, and admire the view. Only four people were present: Major P.A. Curry, Vancouver Mayor Lyle Telford and his wife, and a serving maid. The Queen poured tea, and asked Major Curry if it was possible to buy a home here, as 'this seems to be the place to live.' After a twenty minute stop, the procession resumed, and they headed south, returning to the city over the new Lions Gate Bridge.

A request by the bridge company to have Their Majesties unveil a plaque officially opening the bridge had been denied. Another request to have a curtain in front of a plaque electrically released as they drove past was also turned down. The motorcade never paused, although the Royal Couple were said to have 'honoured' the bridge by driving over it. The one person most responsible for the impressive new developments that the King and Queen had just toured, Fred Taylor, had resigned from the bridge company three days earlier, and had not been invited to any of the official ceremonies. The man from British Columbia who had made all this happen, and whose wife had been presented at court, stood with the crowds beside the road that bears his name as the Royals passed by, on to the CPR dock, where they left by ship for Victoria.

What should have been the happiest time of Taylor's life instead brought depression. In 1939, he travelled to England to set up a new company, British Pacific Development, which would seek investment for the development of Sentinel Hill and the construction of the Garibaldi Highway. Keenly aware of his lack of formal education, he made plans to attend Nuffield College, Oxford. Later that year he returned to Vancouver, but his speculative ventures were put on hold with the outbreak of the Second World War in September. Because of his extensive business

The British Properties Company Cottage.

The one place Taylor's name ever appeared as a public acknowledgement of his role as creator of the bridge was on a dedicatory plaque placed on the west pylon, shown above. This plaque was replaced by the Provincial Government after it acquired the bridge in 1955. The plaque currently on the bridge reads:

THE LIONS' GATE BRIDGE
COMPLETED NOVEMBER 14TH, 1938
DESIGNING AND SUPERVISORY ENGINEERS
MONSARRET AND PRATLEY
ASSOCIATE ENGINEER: W.G. SWAN
CONSULTING ENGINEERS: ROBINSON & STEINMAN
CONTRACTORS: STUART CAMERON & CO. LTD.
DOMINION BRIDGE CO.—HAMILTON BRIDGE CO. LTD.

OWNERS
BRITISH COLUMBIA TOLL HIGHWAYS
AND BRIDGES AUTHORITY

## THE PLAQUES

Not only was Taylor's name removed, Monsarrat's name was misspelled. Another mistake occurs in the other plaque on the west pylon, installed in 1986 to mark the lighting of the bridge; the Earl of Iveagh was not present at the illumination.

connections throughout North America, Taylor was asked by the British government in 1940 to be second in command to Morris Wilson, his long-time friend and President of the Royal Bank who was now serving as head of the British Purchasing Commission in the coordination of British and American factories. During this time Taylor was instrumental in solving a dangerous shortfall in the production of Allied torpedoes, and in expediting the supply of war planes to Britain from Canada and the U.S. He relocated to Washington for several years working as a 'dollar-a-year' man. Taylor's trips across the Atlantic as technical adviser to the British Ministry of Aircraft Production and his connection with Canadian Lord Beaverbrook remain shrouded in secrecy. One of these transatlantic trips involved an urgent trip to Britain, and Taylor hitched a ride in a bomber being delivered from the United States. The unheated craft had no seats, and the long, rough and very cold voyage proved permanently injurious.

His health failing, Taylor returned to Vancouver in 1943, and resumed some of his speculative enterprises, including the development of a subdivision at Gleneagles in West Vancouver. By 1945 he was increasingly ill, and in June he was rushed to New York in a last minute search for an effective treatment. He died of cancer in a New York hospital late on Thursday evening, July 19, 1945. On his deathbed he had requested that his ashes be scattered from the Lions Gate Bridge. A funeral service was held for him in New York, and his remains were cremated. As a final irony, permission had to be obtained from British Pacific to scatter the ashes off the bridge. Morris Wilson made the arrangements, and Mona brought his ashes home. When she got on the train in New York, the porter carrying the box of ashes asked her, 'Should I put Mr. Taylor up on the rack?' She laughed. Returning home for the last time and memorialized as 'the builder of bridges,' Taylor's ashes were scattered from the centre of the Lions Gate Bridge.

Building the bridge had been Taylor's greatest achievement, but the extent of his anguish over what had happened to him personally remained secret. As the Lion sculptures were being assembled, Taylor, in a symbolic act, placed personal mementos inside one of them. His story of the struggle, along with his baby shoes, remain sealed inside that lion to this day.

Fred Taylor, 18 months old.

*Literally hundreds of prominent figures in business and other walks of life in Canada, the United States and in Great Britain—as well as personal friends who were legion—will have learned of the death in New York of Mr. A.J.T. Taylor with profound regret. Possessed of a dynamic personality, a razor-keen mental equipment, a genius for stripping cumbersome detail from the most intricate technical problem, this brilliant native son of Victoria had established an enviable reputation for himself in the world of industry and finance before he was out of his twenties. For a time Lady Luck dealt somewhat harshly with him—often the reward of ambitious enterprise—but found him made of that sterling stuff which accepts rebuffs as a challenge to new endeavour. No temporary embarrassment could lower "Fred" Taylor's sights; from this province he went to eastern Canada, thence across the Atlantic, eventually gravitating to London, where his wealth of engineering knowledge and business acumen soon earned him the respect and confidence of men of vision. He interested them in his canvass of British Columbia, etched in for them the opportunities awaiting the unafraid in this part of the Commonwealth. Thus was he instrumental in bringing that painting to life on the shores of Burrard Inlet in the shape of the famous Lions' Gate Bridge, development of the holdings of British Properties Limited, including a golf course without peer in this part of the Pacific Northwest. During this period of his business activity Mr. Taylor discovered there were not enough hours in the day to satisfy the urge of his active mind and energetic frame. And his personal success this time was invulnerable to Fortune's vagaries.*

*Victoria Daily Times,* July 21, 1945, page 4

THE ROYALS SHRUGGED

ON MAY 29, 1939 when King George and Queen Elizabeth drove over the Lions Gate Bridge to 'honour' it, the Squamish Indian Band had gathered to greet and honour the English monarchs. For four generations their respect for England had not wavered. This meeting of the Royal representatives would bring the English nation and the Indian nation together for the first time. The bridge was an apt symbol for this meeting.

The Squamish Band had requested that the royal entourage stop at the corner of Capilano Road to receive gifts from the delegations who had travelled from around the province. The Squamish Indians had their own Queen to present. Mary Agnes Capilano, first daughter born of the marriage of two previously warring tribes, the Yaculta and the Squamish, was there to meet the royal couple. She was of royal blood and carried the Capilano line. Her Squamish grandfather, who was married to a Native princess of the Nicomen Nation, had tried for years to make peace with the Yaculta Nation. Finally in a two day mediation he had asked his men to hurtle their spears and fire their muskets into the ocean and peace was made. The Squamish chief's son, and the Yaculta chief's daughter married and gave birth to Lixwiut, meaning Great Lady, Leader, and thenceforth known as the Princess of Peace or Mary Agnes Capilano. When she married Hi-Ash Joe, she honoured him with the Capilano name. He became Chief Joe Capilano and Mary became their Queen. Their daughter, Susan, would later marry Johnny Baker, of English and Squamish blood.

It seemed essential that the Squamish and English queens should meet. But the King and Queen's car did not stop. 'Everyone wanted to get in on the act,' remembered Chief Simon Baker, second son of the Baker-Capilano union. 'This was the only time that we could present my grandmother to the Queen, but the car drove past us. Everybody was crowding in front of us so they wouldn't stop. It was terrible for my grandmother.'

Emily Baker added, 'I guess you had to let them know way in advance. You couldn't just ask them when they came.' As the car passed, the King and Queen waved to the crowd gathered where the car was to have stopped, but the royal car drove on to cross the bridge, which had been built on Squamish surrendered land. No one from the Squamish Nation had been invited to take part in the official celebration. Later that day, when the King and Queen were leaving from the CPR dock, they stepped out briefly and the Queen presented Mary Agnes Capilano with a shawl.

140

This was not the first time that the English and their representatives had not stopped for the Indians. From the time of its conception there had been no question that the natives would be moved aside to allow the construction of a First Narrows Crossing. The Federal Order-in-Council of April 29, 1936 that approved the long awaited decision to build the bridge held no jurisdiction over the land it would span. Indigenous rights to the land at the north and south ends of the bridge belonged to the Squamish Indian Band. But no plebiscites were offered to its citizens.

Chief Joe Mathias (right), his wife (left), and his mother, Mary Capilano (centre), waiting to meet the Royals on May 29, 1939. Joe Mathias (1884-1966) became hereditary Chief of the Squamish band after the death of Chief Joe Capilano in 1910. While he was Chief he attended the coronation of two English monarchs, King George V in 1911 and Queen Elizabeth II in 1953.

OFFICE OF THE

INDIAN AGENT

CANADA
DEPARTMENT
OF
MINES AND RESOURCES
INDIAN AFFAIRS BRANCH

PLEASE QUOTE

FILE_____

416 Federal Building,
Vancouver, B. C.
May 30th 1939.

Dear Mr.Rhodes:

     The Indians were naturally most
disappointed that time did not permit Their Majesties
to stop where they had gathered from all parts of
British Columbia to greet their King and Queen.  The
Indians manned their war canoes afterwards to escort
Their Majesties' ship out of the harbour.

     They had made five rings for Her
Majesty the Queen, four of these were of silver and
made for the Royal Princesses, the other one was of
gold for Her Majesty the Queen.   Had the procession
stopped for a few moments they would have asked permission
to present them.

     I presume there is now no opportunity
of presenting these rings to Her Majesty, but perhaps
you can advise me so that I can explain it to the Indians.

     Yours sincerely,

B/DH.

(F.J.C.Ball)
Indian Agent.

E.E.W.Rhodes Esq.
   Royal Visit Committee,
   Vancouver, B. C.

*We much regret the disappointment of the Indians, but upon further enquiry are pleased to learn that arrangements have since been made to have their gifts,—which emanated from the Fort Rupert tribes on the West Coast of Vancouver Island—passed on to Buckingham Palace for presentation to the Princesses there. We can assure you that every effort was made to fulfill the wishes of Their Majesties, and had they desired to stop it would have, of course, been done. We are assured that Their Majesties took particular pains to acknowledge the homage of their Indian subjects, and that in passing them the rate of speed was considerably lowered.*

E.E.W. Rhodes, Honourary Secretary, Vancouver Committee for the Reception of Their Majesties, June 9, 1939

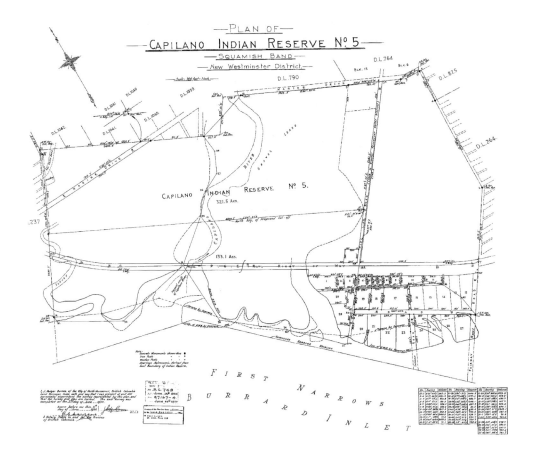

On April 13, 1933, three years prior to federal approval, provincial agreement to construct the bridge had required a survey of the north shore lands to be affected. It had determined that 9.513 acres were needed to provide sufficient access to the bridge. In 1936 the Department of Indian Affairs assessed this land at $3170.00. A valuator fee of $100.00 was added, for a total cost of $3270.00. Formal negotiations to acquire the land began on June 26, 1936 with an application by the First Narrows Bridge Company to the Committee of the Privy Council to surrender for sale 9.513 acres from the Capilano Indian Reserve No. 5. On August 6, 1936, the Minister of Indian Affairs recommended that 'authority be granted to transfer the said lands to the First Narrows Bridge Company, pursuant to the provisions of Section 48 of the Indian Act.' The Committee of the Privy Council concurred.

Negotiations, formal as they were, did not include direct consultation with the Squamish Indian Band. The Department of Indian Affairs, a federal preserve of government officials and documents, did not include nor require Indian representation. An Indian agent appointed by Ottawa was not tasked to represent them. Indian agents at this time, like principals of Indian schools, were mostly retired soldiers from The First World War. Appointed by the federal government, each agent covered many reserves. The Natives never knew who their agent would be. 'He was the boss. He chaired every meeting and told us what's good for us. That's how it was,' said Chief Simon Baker. 'It took us quite a while before we could oppose the agents. Until we got legal advice, all we could do with the land was what the agent said to. They wouldn't let us hire a lawyer. The agent was the lawyer and everything.' The First Narrows crossing would cross the line of authority of the First Nation, yet from the valuation of land to its transfer, the people of the First Nation would not be in the line of authority that gave approval.

More than a decade later, in December, 1947, when an additional 1.63 acres was transferred by Indian agent Henry Edwin Taylor, another surrender for sale from Ottawa again forced the hands of the Chief and principal men of the Squamish Nation. As Native signatories they had no say in the process. Two could not write their names

'We had no say', reminisced Chief Simon Baker. 'We were compelled to surrender the land. The government took over. I couldn't believe what they did. It was done under cover.' In 1936, Baker, then twenty-five, was recently returned from a sojourn off the reservation where he had worked independently for almost a decade. 'The experience taught me what we had to get back.' Six years following the first surrender of land to the First Narrows Bridge Company, Chief Simon Baker would be elected to the Band Council and provide leadership for thirty-three years, from 1942 to 1975, the last ten as manager and chief councillor. 'They got it for a song. It was worth millions even then. If we'd had a good lawyer who could advise us, they never would have built the bridge for that price.'

A much higher price was paid by the Squamish Nation for land lost from the Capilano Reserve. When her husband was on the Band Council, Henry Edwin Taylor was the agent for the Department of Indian Affairs, Emily Baker remembered. 'He would take it to Ottawa, but never do what we wanted. We had no say. He did what they wanted.' What Taylor took to Ottawa in December, 1947 was a 'Surrender for Sale' paper, a document signed by Taylor and the 'Chief and Principal Men' of the Squamish Band, for 1.63 acres of Band

Simon Baker at age 25, as a member of the North Shore Indians lacrosse team. In 1999, when the team was inducted into the B.C. Sports Hall of Fame, Simon was its only surviving member.

land to be added for easement coming off the bridge onto Marine Drive. 'It was taken from us illegally, We are fighting to get that back, Chief Simon Baker stated. 'Like Kitsilano, we will get it back. That was the last they got with their surrender papers. In 1948, we made a motion that says, "We're Indian. We don't sell; we lease." Before 1948 the Indian agent would say, "If you don't sign this, you're going to lose your land anyway. If you sign, you'll get the money." The majority really didn't want to sell but we were convinced that was the only way. As chief councillor I worked for the betterment of our people.' When the Kapilano 100 Committee was struck to negotiate the plans for the Park Royal Shopping Centre, Chairman Chief Simon Baker would ensure that the land was leased rather than sold. After 1948, his conscientious labour would bring revenue from leased lands back to his own people.

Prior to 1948, travel to Ottawa for Band Council chiefs and councillors was often humiliating and futile. Rendered powerless by the orders of government, they could do little to reverse those orders without help from a member of the House. During his tenure as a member of the Squamish Band Council, Simon Baker travelled often to prevent surrenders for sale from reaching the House. "Surrenders for Sale" were a mechanism of the Department of Indian Affairs, for the purpose of transferring Indian lands into private hands. They consisted of pieces of paper on which specific applications were made. Applications for surrenders for sale could be made by anyone via the Indian Affairs' agent. Surrenders would lie in wait of Government House procedure in the order that they arrived. Once dealt with, the deed was done with no recourse for those from whom the lands were taken. Whenever possible, Simon Baker would intercept the surrenders from reaching the floor of the House. 'If you didn't get it out of the pile, it would take a year or more.' Being there at the right time was crucial especially with no representation in the House of Commons. 'Arthur Laing was the only Minister who would phone the clerk and say, "Give the Squamish people their surrender papers." And we got them back,' Chief Baker recalled.

After 1948 there was much more to get back. Lands that had been surrendered and sold officially now amounted to illegal transactions. The documents on which these were registered had to be retrieved and the lands reclaimed. Chief Simon Baker remembered the request to Ottawa for all documents pursuant to Capilano Reserve Lands. The request was granted in part, from 1927 onwards. It was at the behest of Arthur Laing that all the Squamish documents were retrieved by the Baker delegation. Prior to his and Laing's terms of office, much Squamish Indian land had been 'officially' removed from them. ' We had to give land for

Mr. and Mrs. Simon Baker

roads, the PGE Railway, to BC Hydro, for water and sewer.' And the Lions Gate Bridge. Referred to as cut-off lands, there seemed no end to their removal, cutting up the Capilano Reserve land into smaller and smaller segments. Even the house that Chief Capilano had built on Marine Drive was sold and removed in 1960 to become the site of a condominium hotel, The International Plaza. 'He built that so our children would be closer to school. We didn't get very much for it. Was it fourteen thousand?' Emily Baker recalled.

But again, none of this was new. It was reminiscent of the removal of Simon Baker's grandfather's house and garden from a grassy clearing in Stanley Park in 1888. Still known as 'Johnny Baker's Clearing', where the Nine o'clock Gun stands, it was home to Englishman Johnny Baker and his Indian wife Mary Tsiyaliya and their children, until they were told to leave because the first Park Road was being built. 'They used to ask me why I never finished my schooling. I went to the Lytton residential school. We had to work half a day and go to school the other half. I finished grade eight. When I went up to the regular high school in North Vancouver, they said, 'You can't come here. You're Indian,' Chief Simon Baker resumed. 'We'll get it back. That piece coming off the bridge.' And the original bridge land, the 9.513 acres surrendered for $3,170 with an added valuator's fee of $100, to make a grand total of $3,270? 'We could get it back.'

Plans for a new bridge that the Squamish Nation had proposed would require additional Reserve land. That proposal and others that included widening of the bridge had been turned down. Present band policy sends the proceeds from any sale of land directly to a legal fund in Ottawa, which currently holds five million dollars.

Current travel for Chief Simon Baker involves trips to the Supreme Court of Canada. As lifetime honourary member of the Squamish Band Council and Chief Elder, he is chief witness for reclaiming lands illegally taken. The bridge easement leading off Lions Gate Bridge to the east on Marine Drive and leading onto the bridge from North Vancouver is one parcel of land being fought for, along with land on the other side of Burrard Inlet in Kitsilano. 'We got our taxes back, so we'll get our land,' Chief Simon Baker explained. West Vancouver municipality, after leasing property for the Park Royal Shopping Centre, would for many years keep the taxes collected from it. 'We had to fight to get them back.' Tax revenue is divided now, half being sent to the Ottawa fund and half shared by the Squamish Band.

Prior to 1927, Kitsilano had been sold in the same manner as all other lands. The Indian agent arrived with a surrender for sale and said to the twenty families then living on that part of the Reserve; 'You'll lose your land anyway' and 'You'll get the money if you sell.' The majority voted to sell. Each family got $11,000. 'It didn't take long before all of it was gone, in most cases,' Chief Simon Baker sadly remembered. 'They used to throw gold dollars at us poor people.' Baker was a school boy home for the summer when he 'caught one or two.'

Once the sale was done, the families were given no time to move. They were told to clear out immediately as Johnny Baker and Mary Tsiyaliya and their children had been told decades previously. In Stanley Park they had been removed for a road. In Kitsilano it was all for money. Many went to North Vancouver, some to Upper Squamish and Brackendale. One family that qualified for a double share, built a longboat, a canoe that would later be the first to sport an outboard motor.

'If we get Kitsilano back, it's only one of our claims,' Chief Simon Baker said optimistically. Another is the pitch and putt green at Ambleside, the site Chief Simon Baker remembers as his mother's home. 'My mother had a shack at Ambleside. She lived there when she came down. She could see the bridge.' Worth millions, it's currently being bartered for prime Howe Sound land.

Across from Ambleside, the peninsula now called Stanley Park had always been home to many Indians. As early as 1888, many of their homes were lost to give way to Park Road. Chief Supplejack Khahtsahlano's cottage and village at Chay-thoos, First Narrows, now known as Prospect Point, were destroyed to make way for the road as were the Indian villages of Whoi-Whoi at the site now known as Lumberman's Arch. Squamish Indian Lodges around Lost Lagoon gave way, first to the Coal Harbour Bridge in 1888, then to the Stanley Park causeway, starting in l936. Lord Stanley, Governor-General of Canada, officially dedicated Stanley Park in 1889. It had been named after him at his own request. In 1950, a statue to him replaced Chief Supplejack's grave.

'There are things they're going to need to know. We have to make them realize what lands are ours. Stanley Park belongs to us too!' Louis Cordocedo, grandson of Chief Supplejack Khahtsahlano, speaks vehemently. 'We were governed by Indian agents, Indian doctors, Indian nurses and Indian police,' all assigned by Ottawa. 'We couldn't see the doctor of our choice. It was like being a prisoner in your own country.'

Louis Cordocedo came from a pioneer family. His father, Benjamin, was a South American sailor who, at the age of fourteen, arrived in Vancouver on a four-masted barque in 1897. Benjamin fell in love with Katherine Kammonack, the daughter of a Squamish chief. They were considered to be the second family to settle in West Vancouver. Ten of their fifteen children survived, including the youngest, Louis. 'I used to walk over the backs of salmon to cross the Capilano. There used to be that many of them. Since I was six years old I would catch clams and oysters right outside our house. My mother and grandfather could hardly speak English.'

A South American barque *T.V. Kruse* passing under Lions Gate, 1939.

Louis Cordocedo lived in a cedar house built on stilts beyond the PGE on the north shore of the Capilano Reserve Land, beneath the proposed site of the Lions Gate Bridge. 'When bridge work began I had to explain it to our parents. 'It's on Indian land. Are we going to be employed?' There wasn't any talk of the bridge. It was done very quietly. When we wanted to know how wide the bridge would be and how much land it would take, they wouldn't tell us. We had no people, no lawyers. They would just take the land. The contractors moved in and didn't hire any Indians. It was Andy Paull, our Indian Chief who said, 'You can't trespass our land without hiring Indians.' We had to go to court so they would hire us. So they divided the work between the contractor's white workers and said to us, "You can clean the land." Where they built the bridge it was all rock and bush. We had to do the bull work, building fires and clearing, in Stanley Park and under the bridge on the north side. That's how they did it. They let us work. The work lasted less than six weeks. Then we were laid off. I worked cutting the land. Then when they began paving they didn't hire any Indians, only white people. I asked, 'How come they're paving on Indian land and Indians don't get work?' So I got work for two weeks. Then they laid me off. In Stanley Park they paid four people $1,500 each to sell the land. We had no channels. August Jack Khahtsahlano, Dominic Charlie, Jack Lewis and the Moodys had to move. It was a private sale. They moved to Capilano. When the bridge was built they charged a toll and we had to pay to go across. We went to court and after that they didn't charge us. All the money went to the Guinness people who had paid for the bridge. I guess they owned it. But we owned the land and we didn't get a nickel. They stopped the toll when the Guinness people got all their money back.'

'They took all the Indian land in Port Moody for Ioco. My grandfather's land!' says Louis Cordocedo. 'He moved there when his land was taken for the bridge. That's all Indian land. We'll get it back with the land claims,' he adds with a smile. 'That's why the young people have to know what's ours.'

Louis Cordocedo's home, built on cedar stilts, was located in the Indian village on the Capilano Reserve beneath the proposed site of the bridge.

Mr. and Mrs. Louis Cordocedo

148

Marjorie Miranda lived in a shack where the duck pond is now at Ambleside, before being removed to St. Paul's Boarding School in North Vancouver, at age five. 'I couldn't speak any English but I had to. I wasn't allowed to speak my language. I stayed there until I was sixteen. I finished grade eight. There was no other school to go to. We weren't allowed at the white school. I don't know what happened to our shack.' When she married Louis Cordocedo at eighteen, they were turned off the Reservation. Louis' father was non-Indian, giving him non-Indian status. When Louis' father died and left Louis to care for his mother, they lived for a time in the original cedar house underneath the bridge. When she contracted pneumonia, they had to leave their home because one reservation nurse and one doctor could not provide adequate care. They moved off the Reserve to live with Louis' sister who had no Indian status because she had married a blood Chilean.

Once Louis' mother died, he was not welcome on the Reserve. The cedar house that he and his mother had lived in had been dismantled by Isaac Jacobs, a Shaker minister who used the cedar to build a church. Only two cedar posts remain to this day. Eventually, the entire village was dismantled. It did not matter that Marjorie, Louis' wife and soon to be mother of two sons, was Squamish Indian. Before 1985, the government ruled that the male blood line counted and the female did not. The Cordocedos lived off the Reserve until 1985, when Bill C31 finally returned Native status to the matrilineal line, where it had always been in Indian law. They were invited back by the Squamish Band Council and, as elders, were provided with a new home. Marjorie's uncle, Dr. Louis Miranda, a renowned linguist and teacher, had written a scholarly book called *The Squamish Language* published in 1967. She received it as a gift. 'He was a good teacher and he loved it.' Louis Miranda was one of the signatories who had written his name on the surrender for sale of Reserve land, acquired as bridge land, in 1947.

'The Indian agent looked after all our lands. He leased the land on the Seymour River to Smithrite for ninety-nine years at $350 per month. Then Smithrite leased it out to someone else. To get the land back it's going to cost $1.2 million just to get them out,' she says. 'We're fighting for self-government. It's going to take the Indian people a hundred years to learn to take care of themselves,' she adds. 'They have had everything taken away from them, and then everything done for them, disabling them. It's going to take them a long time to learn to do it for themselves.'

IN WITNESS WHEREOF, we have hereunto set our hands and affixed our seals this **19th** day of **December** in the year of our Lord one thousand nine hundred and **forty-seven.**

SIGNED, SEALED AND DELIVERED,
In the presence of

604-770.

Signature Block from Surrender for Sale.

RENEWAL

THE LIONS GATE BRIDGE, as a personal achievement for A.J.T. Taylor, was a success. It had brought him wealth and fleeting fame, but once achieved, he was free. For Vancouverites, it opened new roadways to business and private gain. It also increased the value of leisure time. Business and pleasure mixed well in the new West Vancouver, developing just across the bridge. North Vancouver's industry gained stride. From the start, the bridge was a necessity for those who envisioned a larger city. Inevitably, the use of the bridge surpassed its original capacity, and not long after Taylor's death the bridge required a renewal of vision.

When the bridge opened, it was estimated that it could comfortably handle the vehicular traffic for a city of two million people, assuming that no more than one in seven would drive a car. This was a serious underestimation, especially in the boom years after 1945, when wartime industries, in order to remain in business, turned to the production of consumer goods, including new automobiles. Only fourteen years had elapsed before this dramatic and unanticipated increase in traffic forced the First Narrows Bridge Company to consider a second bridge. In 1952, the two lanes were converted to three, so that one could be used as a passing lane.

*Commenting on accidents on the Lions' Gate Bridge, the other day, Detective-Sergeant Frank Colpitts of West Vancouver, an experienced traffic officer, gave his opinion that the three-lane highway through Stanley Park and over the bridge was more dangerous than a four-way or a two-way road would be. 'People,' he said, 'tend to use the centre lane for passing in either direction.'*

*So far we have been lucky—almost phenomenally lucky. Though the dangerous three-way highway invites accidents, there haven't been many. But traffic over the bridge is increasing with the growth of population on the North Shore and with the ferry services to Nanaimo and Gibsons from Horseshoe Bay. Presently, there will be added the traffic of a new service to Powell River. With all this new pressure, we cannot hope that our good luck will continue.*

*Vancouver Daily Province,* September 23, 1953

SHOPPING · CENTRE · WEST · VANCOUVER · FOR · BRITISH · PACIFIC · PROPERTIES · LIMITED ·

After the war British Pacific Properties decided to tackle a new venture, a shopping centre in West Vancouver. This type of development was quite new in the United States, but hadn't been tried in Canada. Built on land leased from the Squamish Band, this open-air complex on the north side of Marine Drive boasted a row of shops anchored by Woodward's Department Store. It opened in 1950, and has been expanding ever since.

Given the mounting public pressure, it seemed certain that the First Narrows Bridge Company would undertake the construction of a new bridge. By 1953 they were negotiating for eleven acres of Reserve land just east of the existing structure. The planning accelerated dramatically when Premier W.A.C. Bennett became personally involved. Known as an enthusiastic and aggressive highway builder, Bennett had set out to modernize the province's infrastructure after his election in 1952. He recognized the tremendous potential for growth on the North Shore and the need for immediate action.

152

*"What's it worth if we don't snitch on that bit about 'heads a bridge, tails a tunnel and if it stands on end, we fill the ruddy thing in...'"*

*Bennett is inclined to speculate with much evident relish on the change in traffic volume and speed arising out of the proposed high-level highway through West Vancouver and the projected road to Squamish. He believes that within a few years there will be heavy tourist traffic to and from Garibaldi and on into the interior towards Lillooet.*

*These are provincial roads; why not connect them with a provincial government bridge? Altogether, the premier views as shocking, the series of bottlenecks which make traffic difficult in and out of Vancouver.*

*Vancouver Sun*, July 16, 1954

The Park Royal Shopping Centre, C.B.K. Van Norman, Architect, 1948.

Len Norris cartoon, *Vancouver Sun*, February 10, 1955

Negotiations continued in secret between the province and the bridge company. Bennett refused to confirm or deny the rumours that a deal was underway, but the company manager was known to have taken part in meetings in Victoria. The government finally agreed to buy all the shares of the bridge company, and to meet its outstanding obligations. The British Columbia Toll Highways and Bridges Authority acquired title to the bridge in January of 1955, at a cost of $5,959,060. The tolls that had been in place since 1938, were continued so that the Province could recoup its costs.

Public debate began immediately about the adequacy of the Lions Gate Bridge and the possibility of a new one. The existing structure was seen as outdated, old fashioned, and past its prime. A government report released in 1955, considered a twin bridge essential within five years. Another study in 1958, set a target date of 1966, for a new four lane suspension bridge. These reports fuelled the constant and ongoing public debate about a "Third Crossing."

The crossing at Second Narrows was upgraded with the construction of a new six lane high-level bridge that began in 1957, and was completed three years later. This temporarily relieved traffic congestion, but did not significantly address the traffic issues further west. A technologically advanced scheme to span the First

Narrows, designed by Christopher Owtram, was published in the Journal of the Royal Architectural Institute of Canada in February, 1960. Located to the west of the existing bridge, it featured a cable-stayed structure with a 2,000 foot clear span. Two massive angled concrete towers, 790 feet high, supported three superimposed decks of traffic with a total of twelve lanes. The decks were to have been built mainly of reinforced fibreglass. There is no evidence that this highly imaginative scheme was ever taken seriously.

The design of the Lions Gate Bridge has stood the test of time, and spawned two copycat bridges on the far side of the country.
The Angus L. Macdonald Bridge (above) crosses Halifax harbour, and was opened in 1955.
An adjacent span, the A.M. McKay Toll Bridge, was built several years later.

The New Second Narrows Bridge under construction, 1958.

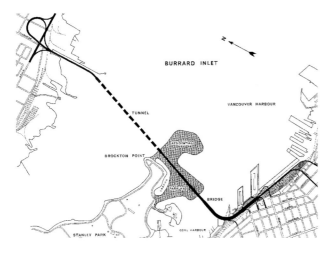

Meanwhile, the Province recouped the purchase price of the bridge and removed the tolls on April 1, 1963; the public had now paid for the bridge twice. Traffic growth continued unabated, and government plans to upgrade the road system grew more grandiose in proportion. A comprehensive new scheme was released that year, designed by Christiani & Nielsen of Canada Ltd. and Foundation of Canada Engineering Corp. Ltd.; McCarter & Nairne were the consulting architects. This was at the height of megaproject planning in British Columbia, and involved the construction of an entire waterfront freeway system, a viaduct leading to a new residential community created by landfill off Brockton Point that would contain half a dozen residential highrises, and a tunnel under the harbour.

The decision to build a Third Crossing seemed imminent, but was continually put off due to shifting political and financial realities. All the while, however, the Lions Gate Bridge was largely ignored, considered an aging relic that did not serve the needs of modern society. One significant traffic and safety improvement was finally made with the installation of lane control signals in 1964, allowing the direction of centre lane traffic to be regulated and reversed.

In 1966 the Burrard Inlet Crossing Report concluded that it was not practical to further increase the capacity of the existing bridge, and recommended the construction of a six lane tunnel at Brockton Point

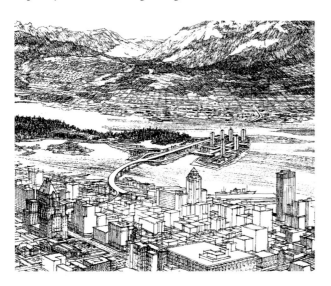

with connections to the Upper Levels Highway and the Georgia Viaduct. Further studies determined the financial and technical viability of such a structure. In 1968, the National Harbours Board retained Swan Wooster Engineering, in partnership with C.B.A. Engineering Ltd., to plan and design the Third Crossing. Two independent design teams were set up, one for a bridge option and and one for a tunnel, each involving freeway connections through Gastown and Chinatown. In 1970 it was recommended that a six lane car and transit bridge be built at the Brockton crossing.

Burrard Inlet Tunnel Crossing, 1963.

There was little doubt that the government was serious this time, but was unable to resolve the issue, as public support for megaprojects was starting to dissolve. Engineers were still enamoured with traffic calculations that showed how Vancouver

could develop a freeway infrastructure equivalent to those being built in major American cities. The development of a postwar automobile culture enabled the explosive growth of new suburban communities, perceived as an idyllic existence based on unlimited mobility. This attitude was on a collision course with a different one developing in the 1960s, a disgust with what the freeway systems in the United States were causing—decaying and unlivable city cores, increasing air pollution, squandering of limited natural resources and sprawling, inefficient cities.

Vancouver was unique in North America in deciding not to follow this trend. In a spectacular triumph of public will, the citizens of Vancouver were successful in stopping the development of a waterfront freeway system that would have destroyed the historic Gastown and Chinatown districts. In a move calculated to halt the freeway, these districts were designated as the Province's first heritage areas in 1971. This effectively halted the proposed construction of the Third Crossing, and signalled that the car would not be the determining force behind future planning for the city.

The Burrard Inlet Bridge Crossing 1970.

*"Let's see, there were the elections of '63, '66, '69, '72, '75, and three
more promised for this one..."*

In the midst of this furor no attention had been paid to the fundamental problems of the Lions Gate Bridge itself, still deteriorating, but considered a low priority. As the bridge had been built with low cost rather than longevity in mind, maintenance needs were paramount, but regular inspections had been curtailed. Shifting provincial politics in the 1970s opened a narrow window of opportunity to repair the failing structure. In 1972 the twenty-year Social Credit regime, famed for its road building and hydro-electric dam megaprojects, was defeated, and replaced by a New Democratic Party administration. This was the year that local bridge engineers Buckland & Taylor were commissioned to investigate the condition and safety of the Lions Gate Bridge. They found it unsafe and in a state of neglect. Significant components required emergency repairs. Corrosion, cable stretching and leaning towers were progressive problems that had to be addressed immediately. The roadbed of the north viaduct was in very poor condition, and individual sidewalk panels had curled from corrosion. After 35 years, the bridge that had been built to carry two lanes of traffic was in fact carrying 60,000 vehicles per day on three lanes. Designed to carry one third of this load, it had taken a severe beating. Immediate steps were taken to avoid further overloading the structure by banning all trucks with a gross vehicle weight over 13,000 pounds.

The bridge also now became a testing ground for new world-wide standards. There were few existing theoretical models for testing traffic, wind and structural loading on a suspension structure. The new wind testing methods were the most sophisticated, and produced ground-breaking results. The traffic study methods were later incorporated into the Canadian Bridge Design Code. As the studies progressed, the structure was found inadequate to resist wind flow. The unexpectedly high load on the cables had pulled the first pier of the viaduct, where the cables bend, out of alignment. Not the least of the problems was the narrow width of the lanes.

In 1975, the entire deck of the north viaduct was replaced in a series of night-time closures. Each night, two old twenty foot long sections of deck were lifted out and a new forty foot section was hoisted into place. The new deck had the sidewalks cantilevered to each side and separated from vehicular traffic, allowing each lane to be widened. A similar deck was designed for the suspension span, with the sidewalks hung outside the stiffening trusses, but this much-needed improvement never went ahead. After only three years in power the NDP government was defeated by the Socred opposition. Plans to continue the redecking were abandoned, although the emergency repairs continued for a time. Further studies were commissioned from Buckland & Taylor, to increase the traffic capacity at the First Narrows, including feasibility studies for double-decking the

Len Norris cartoon, *Vancouver Sun*, September 27, 1963

existing bridge, and for a new, five lane, cable-stayed bridge. Ultimately, no commitment was ever made to the long-term maintenance of the Lions Gate Bridge, as it was firmly fixed in the minds of those responsible that it was inadequate and would have to be replaced.

In 1938 the bridge had been built economically for under six million dollars. By 1979 the emergency repairs had cost eight million dollars, but Buckland & Taylor's work had made the bridge safe and had saved it from total deterioration. The experience would make them leaders in consulting design, training and advice to bridge builders in Canada, the United States, the United Kingdom and China. In 1999, their designs were finally used as the basis for the project that would renew the Lions Gate Bridge.

The rejection of an inner city freeway system did not resolve the regional traffic issues, as the population of the Greater Vancouver Regional District continued to grow. Further strain was put on the existing road system, to the point of collapse. Although not the main bottleneck in the Lower Mainland, the Lions Gate Bridge was targeted for new attention, as it was the most visible symbol of the clash between the old and new vision for the city. Engineering attitudes that had not changed since the 1950s, dictated that a wider crossing would solve the problem.

Thus a new debate began about whether or not the bridge should be swept away in the name of progress. The Ministry's stated intention was to replace the bridge with a larger structure of greater capacity. Symbolic of the unresolved discussion about its future, the bridge continued to deteriorate. Maintenance was shockingly and visibly ignored in anticipation of its demolition. The Ministry also released assessments of the bridge's structural condition that indicated collapse in five years, although careful reading of the studies revealed that only the roadbed was in poor condition. The towers and foundations were actually strong enough to carry up to six lanes of traffic, and it was also technically feasible to convert the existing suspension structure to a cable-stayed configuration.

Preparation of new section of bridge deck, 1975.

Grinding the girder flange clean prior to landing a new section of the bridge deck, 1975.

The Engineering faculty at UBC has a tradition of pulling outrageous stunts every year during Engineering Week. Ten engineers mounted Engineers' Week at UBC in 1982 with more than mundane machismo. They shifted the venue to the unprecedented height of the Lions Gate Bridge. A plan, hatched to strip down and then reinforce a Volkswagen beetle, would unfold over two successive nights. After midnight of the first, two people worked just under the bridge, attaching a cable to its side on the east exposure. Successful, they revelled in their feat well into the night. On the second night, not being caught would be the most sobering thought on each of the participants' minds, at least one of whom was a woman. Long after midnight, scouts positioned at both ends of the bridge, and two hiding beyond the south end into Stanley Park, served as lookouts. None could have predicted what would ensue. Relying on walkie-talkies they thought all communication was completely in their hands. As one person towed the car hitched to a jeep in a somewhat legal manner, onto the bridge from the north end, two others were hidden at the bridge's edge where the cable had been fixed the previous night. No cars were in sight. The beetle was detached, the cable slipped underneath its roof and attached to the side of the bridge, all calculations of weight, tension and strength having been previously

# BUGS ON THE BRIDGE

configured by the masterminds of the plan. Still no cars came. Signalling everyone for every strength possible, the beetle was pushed over the railing with a crash and bang that reverberated in each of the ten pumping hearts fleeing to safety off the bridge. Beneath the beetle which floated in the predawn air, a tugboat pilot shone his light on the swinging sight. 'We couldn't believe that there was no one on the bridge,' recalled one of the 'ten guys.' What they would believe for the rest of their lives is that some greater force other than macho manpower was at work that second night. 'As we were pulling the car, an accident happened in the causeway, stopping all traffic. It was too coincidental. But it wasn't staged.' Not by them.

Getting to bed by dawn, the engineers ventured to view the scene of the crime about noon the following day. A City of Vancouver police horseman appeared in charge below the bridge, looking up at the beetle hanging in mid-air. Eventually a bridge worker was lowered to the car, to hook it onto a cable and winch it onto the bridge. The only damage was a $12,000 removal fee. No reward was tendered for the culprits who scattered their talents over land and sea, never to be caught.

For the 25th anniversary of Engineering Week, in 1994, it was decided to recreate the most famous of the pranks that the UBC students had ever pulled off. One team

poised to hang another Volkswagen Beetle off the Lions Gate Bridge in homage to the famous 1982 stunt.

Two students volunteered to get the cable to the middle of the bridge. Dressed as Ministry of Highways and Vancouver City workers, they hot-wired the maintenance tram, one receiving a tremendous shock in the process. They were finally able to start the tram, and made it successfully to the centre of the span. One of the students had to hang halfway out of the side to throw the cable upwards. The can of spray paint he had in his pocket to mark the location of the cable fell out, and they never even heard it hit the water. Somehow in the darkness they were able to get the cable slung over the edge of the roadbed and up onto the sidewalk.

They took the tram back to the end and walked back to Prospect Point, where a stripped-down Beetle on a flatbed truck and four other students were waiting. They were uncertain at this point whether they would be helped or hindered by two unique circumstances. At the south end of the bridge a work crew had one lane of traffic blocked off, while at the north end a Counter Attack roadblock was slowing down traffic coming onto the bridge. At this time of night the bridge should have been relatively deserted, but on the one night they chose for the stunt there was activity at each end. As the two students joined the group waiting in the parking lot, fire trucks also started to arrive, as

squatters in the park had started a fire, and an alarm had been turned in. Now more rushed than ever, they got the flatbed to the middle of the bridge. The Beetle was balanced on 4 by 4 posts, which they hauled onto their shoulders, intending to launch the car, now connected to the cable, off the timbers. They knew from the experience of the 1982 group and their own engineering knowledge that if they dropped the Bug straight down, the cable would snap. The car had to be swung out from the bridge in an arc that would allow the cable to slowly take the weight as it straightened. As the car started to slide over the railing, one of the timbers broke. The Beetle skewed sideways, and slid to rest, stuck between the railing and the cable structure.

Now panicked, feeling exposed and defeated, some of the students decided to bolt, leaving the two leaders who had hot-wired the tram. The bigger of the two, the one who had received the shock, was not willing to give up. Grabbing one of the timbers, he ran through the traffic across the width of the bridge and lunged screaming at the Beetle, using the post as a battering ram. He hit the car square in the middle and it popped over the railing in a graceful arc, swinging to rest below the bridge just as originally planned. The Bug on the Bridge stunt had been successfully recreated, with the perpetrators uncaught, proving once again the engineering students' tenacity and daring.

Prior to the government's privatization of its management, bridge patrol was the jurisdiction of peace officers. Policing the bridge on Harley Davidson motorcycles, their job entailed a 24-hour call to accidents, stalls, jumpers and unsafe drivers. 'The Harleys were the most efficient way to get through traffic. Our job was to move traffic, not to be supercops,' recalls veteran peace officer Pete Peters. 'When some twit would use the centre lane when it was closed, we would write a ticket. They don't know what counterflow or ambulance may come. It is very dangerous even when the lane change is signalled.'

Today, traffic is monitored on five cameras twenty-four hours per day by Capilano Highway Services' personnel. Dave Howard, Supervisor for Patrol and Communications, has worked through many changes on the bridge. Before the system was computerized in 1994, a manual console was used to manage the traffic. 'To change three miles of traffic in three minutes, it was a pretty efficient counterflow system.' The centre lane change still takes

# BRIDGE PATROL

The Bridge Patrol, circa 1972. Dave Howard is third from the right.

just three minutes, one for the amber warning signal and two minutes for the red signal.

Jody Wonnick has worked as communications officer on the bridge for ten years. 'The hardest part of the job is the shift work.' Rush hours are governed by strict guidelines; the counterflow lanes must remain open in the morning from 6 a.m. to 9 a.m. and in the evening from 3 p.m. to 7 p.m. 'We are not allowed to change the lanes within this time frame. There are better ways to manage traffic at those times. We should have discretionary power,' Wonnick states.

At other times, the call for a lane change can come from the truck operator at the Stanley Park end or from the management officer, depending on the traffic flow. The process takes a total of twenty-one minutes. No traffic stall takes longer than ten minutes to clear. An accident requiring the help of police takes longer.

Dave Howard cites the decorating of the bridge as a high point in his career. 'I was proud. My kids said, 'There's daddy's bridge. all lit up! It

*"Can't understand the significance of their new park decorations but I don't doubt that it's all very authentic Indian legend."*

showed the entrance to one of the most beautiful cities in the world. It was the crowning glory.' The other high point was 'seeing the engineers refurbish the bridge in the seventies. All the work was done at night. Everything was on schedule and the bridge was open every morning at 6 a.m. Given what I saw, I have all the confidence that they will do a great job of refurbishing the bridge again. I'd like to stay around for the final engineering of the bridge. It will be the exciting part of it. I'd like to be here. It will be a new challenge to work through that change.'

Howard's low point of his experience with the bridge is the suicides he has seen. 'It's tragic when someone, for whatever reason, takes his or her own life. It takes a chunk out of you. Nowadays, they are rich, poor, young, old, male, female.

Suicide knows no boundaries. The eldest one I've seen was 87, a man. The youngest was 14, a girl. I'll never get over the suicides. Never. The trauma involved stays with you. You're a human being.'

The lions at the Stanley Park entrance have, of course, had their lions' share of nude models, scavenger hunts and decorations. Until recently, red Christmas bows appeared around their necks mysteriously. Once caught red-handed, the phantom decorator now has to ask permission to dress the kings of Lions Gate.

Dave Howard and Pete Peters on Honda Patrol Bikes, in the 1980s.

Len Norris cartoon, *Vancouver Sun*, September 29, 1964.

Suicide memorial, foot of Lions Gate Bridge.

In 1987 Premier Bill Van der Zalm instituted privatization of highway and bridge maintenance in the province of British Columbia. His proposed scheme gave each employee a chance to share in a group venture. Fledgling groups on Vancouver Island and the southern Gulf Islands didn't fly. A group on the Lower Mainland didn't either. A private proposal from the Drummond family business, now called Capilano Highway Services, did. Previously involved in highway building and construction, once awarded the new contract in 1988 they changed focus to maintenance, with five to ten percent being bridge work. Capilano Highway Services' crews now maintain 140 bridges, of which the Lions Gate Bridge is one, and with it, the Second Narrows Bridge creates their biggest job. Their patrol of Lions Gate provides monitored lane changes and 24-hour service to the bridge. 'It would be great, and less of a worry,' commented Steven R. Drummond, general manager of Capilano Highway Services, on the renewal of the bridge. 'Being handed a new structure should be easier. It will be a new Lions Gate Bridge!'

Drummond's involvement began in 1997 when he was asked to be part of the team called 'Design-Build-Operate.' There was great opportunity, great vision.' His involvement in the operation and maintenance aspects of a brand new bridge would have been assured for thirty years 'if we were successful.' They weren't. The idea of a renewed bridge won out over a new design. Disappointed, 'we were caught in the middle.' As a company situated on Bridge Road immediately underneath the Lions Gate Bridge, 'we didn't want to see someone else doing the work.' When the plan for a renewed bridge was sure, Drummond felt relieved. 'The wider sidewalks separated from the traffic will be a great benefit.' And an enlightened Highways Department is essential for dealing with pedestrians and motorcyclists. As for the lane surface, asphalt was not in the original composition. Years of wear necessitated thin layers of asphalt applied every couple of years to protect the steel grid. Thin layers? 'Because of the added weight.' And the mechanical travellers running end to end beneath the bridge? 'The Ministry will be handling them.'

The bridge remains one of the most heavily used in the Lower Mainland. Every day, between 60 and 70 thousand vehicles pass over the bridge, for a total of 25 million vehicle trips per year.

# BRIDGE MAINTENANCE

In late 1986 I arrived back in Vancouver after living abroad for a year. On that first evening back, I looked down at the bridge and saw that it had been garlanded with brilliant pearls of light along its graceful lines. I was shocked—it was so beautiful it made me catch my breath.

I asked my father about these lights, and he told me they were called 'Gracie's Necklace,' after a local politician. I realized that in the almost five decades since the bridge had been built, the city had been secretly dreaming of the day when it would cloak its bridge in light, and now the dream had become real life.

And I also remember telling my father that the moment they flipped the switch, every house on the North Shore went up in price by $25,000.
Douglas Coupland

The garland of lights hung to celebrate the Province's Expo 86 celebrations was immediately nicknamed Gracie's Necklace after Social Credit MLA Grace McCarthy, who had masterminded the project. She initiated a meeting in London with John Humphreys, a lawyer in a firm long associated with the Guinnesses. It caught the family's imagination, and they agreed to fund the decorative lighting on the bridge as a gift to the City. C.H.E. Williams, the company that provided the bridge's original lighting, was hired to string 170 mercury vapour lights along the catenary suspension cables. The cost of the lighting was paid for by the Guinness family, the original owners of the bridge. On February 19, 1986, the Honourable Erskine Guinness and his wife Louise, attended the official first illumination of the bridge. Erskine was the son of the second Lord Moyne, Bryan Guinness, who had travelled to Vancouver in 1934 as part of the group of 'British Industrialists.' Premier Bill Bennett and Mrs. Guinness fired the ceremonial flares that signalled the lighting of the bridge.

**GRACIE'S NECKLACE**

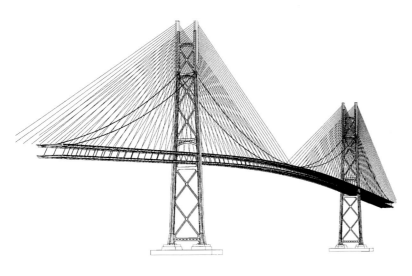

The discussions concerning the replacement of the bridge came to a head in July of 1993, when the Ministry initiated the Choices Program, a provincial task force appointed to determine the most suitable replacement for the existing bridge. Retention of the structure in its existing configuration was not considered an option.

*The more words I read and hear about the current condition and future of the Lions' Gate Bridge, the more confused I become... I cannot understand why one set of engineers state categorically that the Lions' Gate Bridge is falling down and the other says it is both okay and, if given the maintenance envisaged by the original designers, will last a long time. The bridge is a built thing, after all, and the math that created it is still, one presumes, the math that will create the new one.*

Michael Kluckner, 1994

The public debate that followed was rancorous, and pitted those in love with the car against environmentalists, heritage advocates, and neighbourhood preservationists. Similar to the battle against the waterfront freeway thirty years before, the rhetoric was breathtaking. The business community's opinion was generally in favour of bigger and better road systems at any cost (the bridge was dubbed 'The Car-Strangled Spanner') but many others opposed potential impacts to Stanley Park and to the residential areas at each end of the bridge. To paraphrase one argument, increasing traffic capacity in order to solve congestion is the equivalent of loosening your belt to solve obesity—it doesn't address the cause, just the symptoms.

The Heritage Choice was one of the submissions to the Choices Program. Prepared by Roger Bayley, P.Eng. and a team of subconsultants, it retained the essence of the bridge while allowing for six lanes of traffic. The existing suspension structure and roadbed would have been replaced with a new cable-stayed double deck. The towers would have been extended in height, and a three lane tunnel would have been required under the existing Stanley Park causeway. The causeway would have been restored as an historic park drive complete with the original light standards and signage.

A number of speculative schemes were now developed, including six lane replacement structures, and a six lane double-decking of the existing bridge. A Montreal engineering firm, SNC-Lavalin, formed a partnership with the Squamish Band to propose a twin bridge, identical to the existing span, to be built 100 feet to the east. Other more bizarre schemes emerged, including a gondola lift. Even the idea of building a residential island in the harbour to pay for a tunnel was dusted off after thirty years and re-presented.

World renowned local architect Arthur Erickson weighed in heavily on the side of retaining the bridge, but within the context of an upgraded regional traffic network.

*The current proposals that the Highways Minister has endorsed—for upgrading the Lions' Gate Bridge—represent a typically myopic point of view. Both government and the building professions, focussed on isolated issues, are blind to the consequences of their initiatives on the larger picture of Lower Mainland growth. To let this monument deteriorate as it has over the last decade, to have put lights on it instead of what it needed—paint—is a black mark against our governments past and present. That bridge, as one of our few important urban structures, has to be restored, maintained and in no way changed. No other span or structure should be added, no twinning, no lanes above, below or beside; that would be a sad detraction for so handsome a specimen of that period in our history.*
Arthur Erickson, *Vancouver Sun*, April 1, 1997

The circular debate continued, and support for a six lane crossing through the park evaporated. It quickly became apparent that the cost of replacing the Lions Gate Bridge with a four lane structure was wildly out of proportion to the public benefit that could be achieved. As public opinion started to turn against the replacement proposals, suddenly the heritage value and the iconic significance of the bridge was rediscovered by a wider group of citizens. In a stunning reversal of its position, the Ministry finally resolved the issue when it announced, on May 22, 1998, that it was abandoning plans to demolish or significantly alter the Lions Gate Bridge. Instead, it started a process that would lead to the refurbishment of the bridge in its existing three lane configuration.

A renewed Lions Gate was now on the drawing board. The towers and suspension cables would retain the bridge's heritage and history, but everything else would be new. The stiffening trusses would be completely replaced with new, slimmer trusses, above which would sit the new road bed. The deck would be forty percent wider, with the sidewalks cantilevered on the outside of the structure. Plans to improve the causeway through Stanley Park by widening the lanes to match the new standard for the bridge were cancelled. The Vancouver Board of Parks and Recreation, frustrated in its attempts to ban traffic from the park entirely, adamantly refused to allow for one inch of expansion. The Stanley Park causeway would be resurfaced but not widened.

The process of reconstruction involves extensive obstacles to both vehicular and shipping traffic. This is the first time that the entire suspended structure of a bridge will be replaced while traffic continues to use it. The province awarded the $86.5 million refurbishment contract in May, 1999 to the team of Surespan General Contractors, of West Vancouver, and American Bridge Canada Ltd. Other project costs included $12.1 million for project engineering and supervision, and $1.2 million for improvements to Lost Lagoon and Beaver Lake.

On August 3, 1999 the bridge was handed over to the contractors, and work began. Starting in January, 2000, old sections of the bridge deck, including the stiffening trusses, are being cut out, and lowered to a barge, while new sections are hoisted into place. Traffic is carried over the gap on a temporary deck section while work continues below. John Mackie, Navigable Waters Protection Officer, is responsible for work in all waterways in the Western Region. 'The Lions Gate Bridge has not been a big responsibility' he says, but its refurbishment is guaranteed to place more demands on his time. The Navigable Waters Act 'gives four ships sailing under a bridge rights over thousands of commuters riding over it.' Whatever the bridge work, the Act falls under Federal jurisdiction, and must be met, as it was when the bridge was first approved.

What would Fred Taylor have thought of these plans to retain the Lions Gate Bridge? An idealist and a visionary from the beginning, he had originally advocated a bigger bridge, and there is good reason to believe that, were he alive, he would want to be right in there with plans for a larger crossing. Taylor would not have allowed his sentimentality, nor the doubts of others, to stand in the way of what he viewed as progress. Six lanes, which the Lions Gate Bridge is capable of holding, would have been Taylor's way.

Proposed work on the bridge deck, 2000.

The Lions Gate Bridge before (top) and after (bottom) reconstruction of the bridge deck.

# ACKNOWLEDGEMENTS

The idea for a book about the Lions Gate Bridge germinated in the efforts to preserve the bridge when it was threatened with replacement in 1993. It was clear that the bridge was an important landmark, but much of its background, and how and why it was built, remained mysterious. A Lions Gate Bridge Subcommittee was formed under the auspices of the Heritage Vancouver Society, consisting of Donald Luxton; James D. Lowe; Jo Scott B; Eliza Massey; Julie MacDonald; Peter Vaisbord; Mary B. McDonald; Ian Fisher; Barry McGinn; and John R. Stuart. Initial research on the historical significance of the bridge was undertaken by Julie MacDonald. As the Subcommittee continued to agitate for the preservation of the bridge, its complex story, that had never been fully explored, began to emerge.

A book that bridges so many boundaries of time and place would not have been possible without the assistance of many people. The pivotal role of A.J.T. Taylor in the development of Vancouver had been previously neglected. We extend our sincere appreciation to his family for providing information about his fascinating life and his heroic efforts to build the bridge. Taylor's daughter, Joan D. Stockdill, illuminated the story of this remarkable man, and we thank her for the time she spent with us. His son, Peter Taylor, patiently and graciously responded to our questions. Considerable assistance throughout the project was provided by Anthony C. Taylor and Lara Taylor. The story would not have been complete without their generous cooperation, and we hope that we have begun to redress the public neglect of A.J.T. Taylor's accomplishments.

The gracious assistance of Simon and Emily Baker, and Louis and Marjorie Cordocedo, of the Squamish Nation made it possible to tell another side of the story. It was a delight and a privilege to meet them and learn from them. Our thanks go to Gibby Jacobs, Squamish Band Council, and Stefany Mathias, Squamish Band, for getting us on track. Barry Cordocedo merged past and present with a guided tour of ancestral ground beneath the bridge.

Many people helped us in our understanding of the bridge itself, including Peter Buckland of Buckland & Taylor Ltd.; S. Anthony Toth, President, B.C. Road Builders and Heavy Construction Association; Roger Bayley, P.Eng., Paul Merrick Architects; Sonya Polowy, Human Resources Assistant, Sandwell Engineering Inc.; John Mackie, Navigable Waters Protection Officer; Peter Humphrys, Natural Resources Canada; Colin Parkinson, Coast Guard, and Andrew Todd. Henry Evanisky, Lions Gate Bridge Maintenance/Inspection Technician, Ministry of Transportation and Highways, provided a real 'nuts and bolts tour' of the bridge that was a rivetting experience! The staff of the Capilano Highway Services have generously shared their time and experience, including Steven R. Drummond, General Manager; Pete Peters, Dave Howard, and Jody Wonnick, Communications Officers. For providing original plans of the bridge, and for guiding us through the current plans for its renewal, we thank Geoff Freer, Project Director, John Doyle, Director, Communications and Public Affairs, and Ian Druce, Communications Manager, of the Lions Gate Project, Director, B.C. Transportation Financing Authority.

Much of the story was contained in local archives. We were blessed with the enthusiastic assistance of the staff of the North Vancouver Museum & Archives; Francis Mansbridge, Archivist, June Thompson, Assistant Archivist; Cecil Halsey, Photography Technician; and Robin Inglis, Director. Our sincere thanks are also due to Carol Haber, Ann Carroll, and the staff of the City of Vancouver Archives; Sue Camilleri Konar and the staff of the Vancouver Public Library; Preben Mortensen, Community Records Archivist, West Vancouver Museum & Archives; George Brandak,

Head, Special Collections, University of British Columbia; Gene Bridwell, Special Collections, Simon Fraser University; and Diane Rogers, Jewish Historical Society. Clarification on the role of the Guinness family was provided by Gerald McGavin, Chairman and Chief Executive Officer, British Pacific Properties Ltd., and Anthony Laoun, President, Duke Seabridge Limited. Peggy Imredy, whose primary research on Charles Marega has kept his memory alive, verified information that we have included in this book. Additional photographs were located through the kind assistance of Eric Pattison, the son of Ken Pattison of Photocraft; Esmée Mansell, the daughter of Fred Laughton Townley; and Clara S. Coles, daughter of architect William Bow. Cheryl Loukas, Buckland & Taylor Ltd. and Casey Tuerlings, Sandwell Engineering Inc. helped provide key images. Eliza Massey provided compelling contemporary photography.

Unravelling this complex story has been a challenge. We were assisted by David Monteyne, whose meticulous research resolved many unanswered questions. For assistance in locating far-flung archival material, we are indebted to Karen Mann, London; Donna Jean MacKinnon, New York; David Jehn, New York; Bruce Forster, Vancouver; Mrs. D.M. Forster, West Vancouver; Mr. James V. Reed, Archives Center, Rockefeller Center, New York; Sarah Montgomery, National Archives of Canada; Mary Ann Bamberger, Asst. Special Collections, Librarian/Associate Professor, University Library, University of Chicago at Illinois; and Geri Jones, P.R. & Marketing Assistance, Earls Court Olympia, London. For assisting in the search for information about the elusive John W. Wood, we acknowledge the assistance of Mary Lamoreux, Ordre des Architectes du Québec, Montreal; Robert Hill, Toronto; Gordon Fulton, Ottawa; Susan Bronson, Montreal; Michèle Picard, Secretary, Docomomo Quebec; Judy Scott, Royal Architectural Institute of Canada, Ottawa; Paul Chénier, Canadian Centre for Architecture, Montreal; and Sandra Cohen-Rose, Montreal.

We would also like to acknowledge the assistance of Douglas Coupland; Jim Sutherland, Editor-in-Chief, Vancouver Magazine; Berna E. Ho, Office Administrator, Goodman, Phillips & Vineberg, Vancouver Office; Philip Parker; Jeannette Hlavach, Senior Heritage Planner, City of Vancouver; and a special thanks to John Wellwood, for his helpful advice.

The production of this book has been a team effort. Leon Phillips, graphic designer, has translated our thoughts and ideas into a transcendent design, with loyalty to content and coherence through countless revisions. We are grateful for the opportunity to have worked with the team at Talonbooks, not only for their belief in this project but for also making it enjoyable. Their support has been invaluable; our sincerest thanks go to Karl Siegler and Christy Siegler, for inspiration, editing, guidance and advice; and to Shyla Seller and Lori Emerson for their efforts on behalf of this project.

Three people, no longer with us, laboured to preserve the history of the Lions Gate Bridge, and deserve special mention. Leonard Frank, well-known Vancouver photographer, captured many superb images of the bridge under construction. David Loughnan, a manager at Spencer's Department Store, chronicled the progress of the bridge both through his photographs and his detailed notes. Major James Skitt Matthews, the founder of the City of Vancouver Archives, recognized the historical importance of the bridge and went to great lengths to collect primary material about its construction. We owe a debt to their labours, which have preserved for posterity the legacy of Lions Gate.

# REFERENCES

A NOTE ON SOURCES

The Lions Gate Bridge was a matter of public interest and debate for decades, and no one source begins to tell its full story. Our investigation included a review of hundreds of individual references, far too extensive to list, and a decision was made to eliminate footnotes in the body of the text.

The bridge controversy and construction occurred within the memory of many still alive, and the personal interviews we conducted were an invaluable source of information. Countless newspaper articles were published, almost daily, in the *Vancouver Sun,* the *Vancouver Daily Province,* and the *Vancouver News-Herald,* many of which were collected by Major Matthews, available in scrapbooks at the City of Vancouver Archives. The *Sun* and the *Province* held opposing points of view on the bridge issue, and often employed wild hyperbole and exaggerated claims to support their biases. A great deal of contradictory information had to be assessed, and our interpretation is based on a reconstruction of the most likely events.

We were privileged to be allowed access to many of the documents held by the Taylor family. The Leyland Papers at the West Vancouver Museum & Archives were a valuable source of primary material. Other sources too numerous to mention were used to corroborate individual facts and statements. While many archivists and historians have helped us along the way, we take full responsibility for any errors or omissions.

PUBLISHED SOURCES

Akrigg, G.P.V. and Akrigg, Helen. *British Columbia Place Names.* Vancouver: UBC Press, 3rd Edition, 1997.

Allwood, John. *The Great Exhibitions.* London: Studio Vista, 1977.

Banks, S.R. *The Lions' Gate Bridge.* Montreal: The Engineering Institute of Canada, 1942. Reprinted from *The Engineering Journal,* April, May, June, July 1942.

Buckland, Peter G. *The Lions Gate Bridge: Engineering Innovations.* Vancouver: *The BC Professional Engineer,* March 1984: 8-11.

Burkinshaw, Robert K. *False Creek: History, Images, and Research Sources.* Vancouver: City of Vancouver Archives Occasional Paper No. 2, 1984.

Carroll, Ann. G*uide to Pre-1940 Architectural Records of Vancouver.* Vancouver: City of Vancouver Archives, 1986.

Chisholm, Anne, and Davie, Michael. *Beaverbrook: A Life.* London: Hutchinson, 1992.

Christiani & Nielsen of Canada Ltd. & Foundation of Canada Engineering Corp. Ltd. *Burrard Inlet Tunnel Crossing.* Vancouver: 1963.

Cockfield, Brown and Company Limited. *Report on Traffic and Earnings of Proposed First Narrows Bridge.* Montreal, Toronto, Winnipeg, Vancouver: 1934.

Coupland, Douglas. *This Bridge is Ours.* Vancouver: *Vancouver Magazine,* Vol. 27 No. 2, March 1994: 26-30.

De West, Frank. *Vancouver's Lions' Gate Bridge. Authorized by the Lions' Gate Bridge Company Ltd.* [sic]. West Vancouver, Published by Frank De West, 1938.

Dempster, Eleanore. *The Laughing Bridge: A Personal History of the Capilano Suspension Bridge.* Maple Ridge: Impressions in Print Enterprises, 1988.

Division of Information. *America Builds: The Record of PWA.* Washington: United States Government Printing Office, 1939.

*Earl's Court Boasts "Flexible" Pool, Mobile Seating.* Architectural Record, May 1938: 71-73.

Edwards, Gregory. *Hidden Cities: Art & Design in Architectural Details of Vancouver & Victoria.* Vancouver: Talonbooks, 1991.

Fetherling, Doug. *Vision in Steel 1882-1982: One Hundred Years of Growth, Dominion Bridge to AMCA International.* Montreal: AMCA International, 1982.

First Narrows Bridge Company. *Lions Gate Bridge: Vancouver Canada, Souvenir Booklet.* Vancouver: First Narrows Bridge Company Ltd., 1939.

Fitzgerald, Dennis. *The Properties.* Vancouver: *Western Living,* November, 1985.

Foundation Group Designs Ltd. *West Vancouver Heritage Inventory.* District of West Vancouver, 1987-1988.

Harris, Robert C. *A History of the Lions' Gate Bridge, First Narrows, Burrard Inlet, Vancouver, B.C.* Unpublished. Buckland & Taylor Ltd., 1991.

Hayes, William A. *Beaverbrook.* Don Mills, Ontario: Fitzhenry & Whiteside, 1979.

Imredy, Peggy. *A Guide to Sculpture in Vancouver.* Vancouver: 1980.

Johnson-Tekahionwake, E. Pauline. *Legends of Vancouver.* Kingston, Ontario: Quarry Press, 1991.

Kirkness, Verna J., ed. *Khot-La-Cha: The Autobiography of Chief Simon Baker.* Vancouver: Douglas & McIntyre, 1994.

Kluckner, Michael. *The Lions' Gate Bridge—Opinion.* Vancouver: *Heritage Vancouver Newsletter,* February 1994: 1.

———. *Vancouver: The Way It Was.* North Vancouver: Whitecap Books Ltd., 1984.

Loughnan, David. *The Second Narrows Bridge, North Vancouver, British Columbia: Official Opening November 7, 1925.* North Vancouver: 1925.

Macdonald, Bruce. *Vancouver: A Visual History.* Vancouver: Talonbooks, 1992.

Marks, Robert W. *The Dymaxion World of Buckminster Fuller.* Carbondale & Edwardsville: Southern Illinois University Press, 1960.

Matthews, Major James Skitt. *Early Vancouver.* Seven Volumes. Unpublished manuscript.

———. *The Naming, Opening and Dedication of Stanley Park.* Vancouver: City Archives, 1959.

Monteyne, David. *Spider Web of Steel: The History of the Lions Gate Bridge.* Vancouver: City of Vancouver, 1998.

Mullally, Frederic. *The Silver Salver: The Story of the Guinness Family.* Toronto: Granada Publishing Ltd., 1981.

Newspaper Cartoonists Association of B.C. *British Columbians As We See 'Em 1910 and 1911.* Vancouver, 1911.

*£1,250,000 Plan to Make Earl's Court the World's Largest Centre for Exhibitions: A Pictorial Forecast.* London: The Illustrated London News, July 20, 1935: 134-135.

Pawley, Martin. *Buckminster Fuller.* New York: Taplinger Publishing Company, 1990.

Ramsey, Bruce. *A Place of Excellence: A Chronicle of West Vancouver 1912-1987.* Corporation of the District of West Vancouver, 1986.

Scott, Jack. *Suburb in the Sky.* Toronto: *Maclean's Magazine,* November 15, 1948: 20-21, 29, 31.

Shapiro, Mary J. *A Picture History of the Brooklyn Bridge.* New York: Dover Publications Inc., 1983.

Shaw, Charles Lugrin. *Spider Web in Steel: Vancouver's Lions' Gate Span is the Longest Suspension Bridge in the British Empire.* Toronto: *Maclean's Magazine,* August 15, 1938: 13, 33-34.

Short, C.W. and Stanley-Brown, R. *Public Buildings: A Survey of Architecture of Projects Constructed by Federal and Other Governmental Bodies Between the Years 1933 and 1939 with the Assistance of the Public Works Administration.* Washington: United States Government Printing Office, 1939.

Smith, Debbie. *Lions' Gate Bridge Information Manual.* Prepared for Regional Highways Engineer, Ministry of Transportation & Highways, Province of British Columbia, 1979.

Smithells, Roger. *A Home in the Sky.* London: *Decoration,* The Mayfair Press Ltd., Number 16, August, 1936: 8-13.

Massey, Eliza. *Suspense Bridge.* Unpublished Manuscript, 1993.

Stockdill, Joan Drummond. *Biography of A.J.T. Taylor.* Unpublished Manuscript.

———. *The Lions' Gate Bridge—the Great Canadian Bridge Game.* British Columbia Historical News. In two parts: v.9 n.4, June 1976: 16-28; v.10 n.6, November 1976: 18-28.

Swan Wooster-C.B.A. *Notes on the Burrard Inlet Crossing Project: Approaches for the City of Vancouver: Examination of Alternative Concepts.* Vancouver, 1968.

———. *Notes on the Burrard Inlet Crossing Project City of Vancouver Approaches: Final Examination of Alternative Alignments.* Vancouver, 1969.

———. *The Burrard Inlet Crossing: A Report to the National Harbours Board.* Vancouver, 1970.

Taylor, A.J.P. *Beaverbrook.* New York: Simon and Schuster, 1972.

Taylor, G.W. *Builders of British Columbia: An Industrial History.* Victoria: Morriss Publishing, 1982.

Vancouver Town Planning Commission. *Report on Proposed First Narrows Bridge.* Vancouver: December 11, 1933.

*Vancouver's Golden Jubilee 1886-1936: Official Pictorial Souvenir Program.* Lithographed by the *Vancouver Sun,* 1936.

Van der Zee, John. *The Gate: The True Story of the Design and Construction of the Golden Gate Bridge.* New York: Simon & Schuster, 1986.

Walden, Phyllis Sarah. *A History of West Vancouver.* Unpublished MA Thesis, Department of History, UBC, October, 1947.

Williams, David Ricardo. *Mayor Gerry: The Remarkable Gerald Grattan McGeer.* Vancouver: Douglas & McIntyre, 1986.

Windsor Liscombe, Rhodri. *The New Spirit: Modern Architecture in Vancouver 1938-1963.* Vancouver and Montreal: Canadian Centre for Architecture, and Douglas & McIntyre and MIT Press, 1997.

Zuehlke, Mark. *Scoundrels, Dreamers & Second Sons: British Remittance Men in the Canadian West.* Vancouver: Whitecap Books, 1994.

FILMS

*Construction of the Lions' Gate Bridge* [silent film with captions]. Photographed by the Whitefoot Studio, Vancouver. Produced by Stuart Brown of Home Oil Dist. Ltd. and John Anderson of British-Pacific Properties Ltd., 1937-1939.

*A City's Bridge* [video recording]. Produced and directed by James Groundwater; writers, Rachel Preston, Gail Johnson, Pramjit Mahli. Vancouver, 1993.

*Interview with Rex Banks* [video recording]. 1980. North Vancouver Museum and Archives #9385.

# ILLUSTRATIONS

# INDEX

174